Music and the Cultural Production of Scale

Phil Dodds

Music and the Cultural Production of Scale

Phil Dodds
Lund University
Lund, Sweden

ISBN 978-3-031-36282-8   ISBN 978-3-031-36283-5   (eBook)
https://doi.org/10.1007/978-3-031-36283-5

Cover illustration: Pattern © Harvey Loake

This Palgrave Macmillan imprint is published by the registered company Springer Nature Switzerland AG.
The registered company address is: Gewerbestrasse 11, 6330 Cham, Switzerland

ACKNOWLEDGEMENTS

I am grateful to Lund University's Department of Arts and Cultural Sciences for supporting my postdoctoral project on Sonic Sense of Place (2019–2021), and for a research grant from the Swedish Research Council for my project on Musical Colonisation (2022–2025). I came to Lund University as a cultural and historical geographer who happened to research music, so I want to thank my colleagues here in the Division of Musicology for welcoming me and for offering me wise advice during the writing of this book. Special thanks are due to Sanne Krogh Groth, Tobias Lund, Katja Heldt, Anders Reuter and Thomas Olsson for reading and commenting helpfully on different sections of the book. For other tips and suggestions, I am indebted to many other colleagues in Lund, not least Naoko Takayanagi, Brandon Farnsworth, Carin Graminius, Ellen Suneson, Robert Willim, Mikael Askander and Heidrun Führer. All the members of the Aesthetic Studies Reading Group and the Popular Culture Studies Research Node helped me develop my ideas too.

To the archivists at the Moravian Church Archive and Library in London and at the John Rylands Research Institute and Library in Manchester: thank you for all your help with finding collections and for the valuable service you provide. I must also thank students at the Bader International Study Centre and at Lund University for discussing with me and helping me to better understand several of the examples contained in this book. It was often through the teaching process that I came to see some of the key connections between apparently disconnected musical genres, practices and histories. Thanks are also due to Daniel Frost for specific literature recommendations, and to Sam Richardson for expert musical advice. My editor at Palgrave, Robin James, helped me appreciate both the strengths and the weaknesses of my initial ideas for the book, and the final version is much stronger because of her early comments. I also owe thanks to Robin for her support and patience towards the end.

My family have also been unfailingly supportive and patient over the years, so I am incredibly thankful to them all too. And finally, to my partner Lettice: thank you for listening to music with me, for your continuous encouragement and for the amazing intellectual example you set.

CONTENTS

CHAPTER 1

Introduction

Abstract Scales are neither natural nor neutral but actively and constantly produced and practised, with real political effects. Human-geographical and anthropological scholarship has demonstrated this with special attention to political-economic and social processes, but the project of understanding how cultural practices produce scale remains unfinished. A review of music research shows that it tends to use scalar categories (e.g. local, urban, regional, global, world) in varyingly critical ways, and as a field it therefore has both most to gain from and most to offer to a fuller conceptualisation of the cultural production of scale. In particular, music scholars should treat scales as open questions, and as phenomena potentially produced through musical practices, rather than as stable categories upon which to base, or with which to frame, other arguments. Attending to how music harnesses, manipulates, contests and constructs the scales that have been more commonly used to frame and explain it enables a richer musicological analysis and a deeper understanding of the world's geographies.

Keywords Musicology • Scalar categories • Geographical scale • Music geographies • Popular music studies

© The Author(s) 2023   1
P. Dodds, *Music and the Cultural Production of Scale*,
https://doi.org/10.1007/978-3-031-36283-5_1

1.1   THE SCALE OF MUSIC STUDIES

Scales are sets of spatial frames, abstractions or categories that denote the size, proportion, level, extent or hierarchical relations of phenomena. They are, like other frames, abstractions and categories, neither neutral nor natural but politically contested and actively produced through a range of political-economic, social and cultural practices. They are not just *there*. They are *made*. Foundational work by Neil Smith (1992, 1995, 1996, 2010 [1984]) and Sallie Marston (2000; see also Marston et al., 2005) has shed light on the multi-scalar system produced by capitalism, and on the role of complex and gendered patterns of social reproduction and consumption in the constitution and reconstitution of scale. The insights of this human-geographical scholarship have been fruitfully adapted by the anthropologist Anna Tsing in her various studies of scale-making projects, scalar 'conjurings' and (non-)scalability (Tsing, 2000, 2005, 2012). However, the project of understanding how cultural practices produce scale remains unfinished. Smith's (1992, 1996) illustrative work on the scalar functions of specific conceptual art pieces has not been substantially built upon for other areas of cultural activity.

With this book I want to offer a deeper understanding of how scale is culturally produced. I hope to contribute, in doing so, to the research on scale and scale-making in the fields of human geography and cultural studies. I believe this to be an important area of research because I agree with Smith (1992, 62) that the production of scale is 'a primary means through which spatial differentiation "takes place"'. I aim to make this contribution to what might be called 'scale studies' by focusing on music and asking: *how does music produce scale?* I choose music for two main reasons. First, because, as Kirstie Dorr puts it succinctly, 'sonic production and spatial formation are mutually animating processes' (Dorr, 2018, 3), and, moreover, because musicians are often expert practitioners of what Alistair Fraser (2010) has called 'scalecraft' (or 'the craft of scalar practices'). Musicians demonstrate 'the skills, aptitudes, and experiences involved in producing, working with, or exploiting geographical scale' (Fraser, 2010, 334). I will expand on this point in the following chapters, but suffice to note here that musicians are both required to and skilled at working at multiple scales simultaneously, with the facility to produce (and reproduce) recordings and performances that may be heard and repurposed for different sizes of audience in different kinds of places, and to 'conjure' (to use Tsing's [2005] term) the intimate and the universal, or the global *with* the personal. They must keep constantly in mind the scale(s) of their audience, or what Diana Brydon refers to as the challenges of 'meaning-making across different scales of engagement', each of which produces 'its own scales of relation' (2016, 43–44). Most straightforwardly, musicians pursuing professional careers are generally required to produce 'scalable' work (i.e. musical recordings or performances that can be reproduced and circulated in relatively stable formats). They are also involved in the kinds of creative, artistic practices that require sensitivity to the complex scalar textures and interconnections of the world—what Anna McCarthy (2006, 43) calls the 'conjunctures [that] are formed between different "levels" of social life'. Musicians make aesthetic and lyrical choices about the scale of the themes and moods they express. Compare, for example, the intimate soundscape and whispered, breathy vocals of Olivia Rodrigo's record-breaking hit 'Drivers License' (2021) with the more epic choruses of ABBA's 'The Winner Takes It All' (1980). Both are in major keys, in the Western pop music tradition, between four and five minutes long, with lyrics focusing on the breakup of a romantic relationship, addressed in the second person to a former lover. But one sounds clearly 'bigger' than the other. This is in part because musicians may expertly deploy a range of performance, recording and production techniques to produce musical and vocal sounds ranging from the 'very very small' to the 'very very big' (Sofia Jannok quoted in Diamond, 2007, 27)—even when the volume at which we hear them remains the same—as well as specific musical methods for connecting and seguing between these. (I analyse some of these methods in the following chapters). Contemporary pop production software and practice involves working with 'infinitesimal digital details' (Reuter, 2022a, 122) and 'interrelated macro-synthesis of sounds where adjustments multiply across microcosm and macrocosm' such that artists like Billie Eilish are 'constantly producing changing relations of nearness' (Reuter, 2022b, 61; 66). Besides this, musicians are in the business of reinforcing hegemonic conceptions of the relationship between the particular and the universal, or in producing alternative imaginations of differently scaled worlds, which means their work can affect the real scales of social life. This ability of music to (re)produce scales is the central focus of this book.

The second reason for focusing on music here is that academic studies of music have both (a) *most to gain from* and (b) *most to offer to* a fuller conceptualisation of the cultural production of scale. Examples of (b)— where musicological studies can help with understanding scale construction—are highlighted in the following chapters. But first let us focus more closely on (a).

Scale frames music research more than other areas of cultural studies. Scalar categories have long been a stable feature of—and a vexing presence in—research in the broad fields of musicology, ethnomusicology, popular music studies and music geographies. In his 1991 *Cultural Studies* article summarising 'The Music Industry in a Changing World', Will Straw highlighted the challenge of the 'Global' for musicology, as well as issues to do with 'musical practices unfolding within particular urban centres', 'local musical cultures' and 'regional and national musical space'—all on the first page (Straw, 1991, 368). Terms like 'local' and 'global' have been near-ubiquitous in music research since such scholars as Lily Kong popularised them in articles with titles like 'Popular music in Singapore: exploring local cultures, global resources, and regional identities' (1996; see also Kong, 1997). Kong has of course criticised the historical musicological tendency to deploy scalar metaphors merely for 'delimiting areas that share certain musical traits' (Kong, 1995, 185). But the use of scale in musical analysis is often problematically connected to what Dorr (2018) calls 'the "music in place" premise', whereby '"the local" is offered as a spatial metaphor for the ostensibly culturally and geographically fixed or static landscapes of the non-West'—a proxy for the trope of 'rootedness' (Dorr, 2018, 4–5).

When used uncritically, these scalar frames tend to function as relatively stable categories or explanatory factors for how music works—or even, in the cases of 'urban' and 'world' music, to denote entire (and often entirely disconnected) genres.[1] Commonly, 'local' music (generally understood as confined to or inflected by some specific place) is purportedly counter-posed with or affected by a 'bigger', 'global' music culture that circulates placelessly, perhaps via 'extra-local (global) pipelines' (see, e.g., Makkonen, 2015). We see this especially in studies of 'local music policies' in relation to 'the global music industry' that highlight the importance of 'developing an infrastructure that can help and benefit from this local talent as it moves towards the global centre' (Brown et al., 2000, 449; see also Watson, 2008). This account, of 'local' music places seeking to tap into a bigger 'global' music industry explains, for Brown et al. (2000), the status

---

[1] On the politics of 'world music', and attempts to denaturalise the term, see Guilbault (1993) and Feld (2000). On the related issue of 'world' versus 'global' sound art, see Groth (2020).

of a city like London as a 'national/global music city' as opposed to the local/regional centres of northern England. Music theory even uses scalar metaphors to describe 'global keys', 'local tonics' and 'tonal regions' (see, e.g., Lerdahl, 1988). These are just a few examples of how music is conceptualised in music research along a scale ranging, in Jennifer Lena's (2012, 11) words, 'from the hyperlocal to the global', in a way that is barely related to literal spatial extent. Indeed, scalar terms and categories do a lot of work in music research, and my hope is that this book can help enrich musicology by encouraging a more critical engagement with scale.

Connell and Gibson (2003), in their helpful engagement with the 'question of scale', point in this direction. They acknowledge music scholars' attempts to employ both conventional and unconventional scalar abstractions, before asserting that 'more active terms are needed than "global" and "local" or variants such as "glocalisation", which reify the status of geometric space over the dynamic conditions under which space is actively constructed and consumed' (Connell & Gibson, 2003, 17). Some scholars have acknowledged that the scalar complexity of music makes it difficult to apply the terms like 'local', 'regional' and 'global' uncritically (see, e.g., Harris, 2000, 26). Conceptualisations of musical 'communities' and 'collectives' have had to address differing (re)definitions of the 'local' and the 'global' (e.g. Shelemay, 2011). Arun Saldanha is one of many scholars who have attempted 'to map both the "local" and "global" character of young people's musical practices' (2002, 341), but his account—whereby the 'rich kids' actively *perform* a politicised 'global' identity in relation to 'the local other' (ibid.)—is notably rich. Research on music 'scenes' has long grappled with scalar adjectives, sometimes juxtaposing 'local scenes' with 'global networks' (e.g. Dunn, 2016), or reasserting the significance of 'regional music scenes' and 'local accents' of music in specific cities in a context of 'resistance to globalization' (e.g. O'Connor, 2002), or using terms like 'translocal' to account for the spatial complexity of niche scenes, especially when the internet is involved (see, e.g., Kruse, 2010; Bennett & Peterson, 2004; Futrell et al., 2006; Taylor, 2012). 'Glocal' is deployed, too, especially to explain 'local' variations in 'global' genres. But even if a term like 'glocal' might help describe, for example, the 'recontextualization of cultural forms through "local" appropriations of a globally acceptable cultural model' in the world's varied hip-hop communities (Morgan & Bennett, 2011, 181; see also Omoniyi, 2006), it does not explain why the local-to-global scalar system persists as a prevailing analytic lens. In fact, even in music research that makes 'scale(s)' the analytical focus, a relatively stable set of abstractions tend to be used (see, e.g., Westinen, 2014 on global, national and local authenticity in Finnish hip-hop). This is true even when the music being studied in fact explicitly challenges or unsettles the scale of the spatial units in which they are conceived, such as nations across state borders (Hamelink, 2016) and 'nations within nations' (Dunbar-Hall & Gibson, 2000). And even when scalar categories' deficiencies are acknowledged, scales themselves, and the processes of their production and naturalisation, are rarely directly in focus. The question *what does music do to scale?* remains unaddressed.

What is required, following Tsing (2000, 347), is for music researchers to adopt 'Scale as an Object of Analysis'. Music scholars should, I suggest, treat scales as open questions, and as phenomena potentially produced *through* musical practices, rather than as stable categories upon which to base, or with which to frame, other arguments. They should not only ask: which, from this set of spatial frames, should I use to contextualise this music? Instead, they should find it interesting and productive to ask: how does this music produce these sets of spatial frames? I propose, then, to study scales *through* music rather than scales *of* music. This means not using scales to analyse music but exploring music's potential to analyse, use, subvert and produce scales. I seek a richer musicological analysis, and a deeper understanding of cultural-geographical processes more generally, by attending to how music harnesses, manipulates, contests and constructs the scales that have been more commonly used to frame and explain it.

This book focuses on four examples of scalar processes as practised through music. My own archival research, empirical fieldwork findings and musicological analyses inform the arguments I develop, but I also highlight existing work that has shed light on musical scale production. The different chapters address different genres, styles and forms of music, taking in live performances, studio recordings and historical descriptions of music in such diverse contexts as urban neighbourhoods, climate protests, antifascist demonstrations and colonial encounters. The examples may seem disconnected, but the idea is to draw on and across different kinds of 'musickings' (Small, 1998; see also Moisala et al., 2014) and different kinds of 'listening assemblages' (Duffy, 2017) to illustrate several key points about musical scale production. The chapters are also ordered, with a thread that connects them, as I want to explore first how music often works through a shared understanding of musical conventions, but that the establishment and extension of that shared understanding is itself a musical process of 'scaling up' or, in Tsing's terms, producing 'scalability'. In selecting scale as the subject rather than the frame of cultural analysis, I follow Olli Pyyhtinen's call 'to ditch the method of zooming in and zooming out that goes with the shift of perspective' that the local-global or 'micro to macro binary' entails (2017, 303). And instead of structuring the article according to pre-determined and 'precision-nested' scales ranging from the (micro-)local through the regional to the global or universal (see Tsing, 2012), the following sections instead each focus on different scalar processes—different musical means of making and unmaking scales and their connections—that could potentially work at (or between) any scale(s). To begin, though, I explain in greater detail what scale means and what it does by reviewing key literature on scale production, before highlighting in particular those studies that shed light on the cultural production of scale.

1.2   TOWARDS THE CULTURAL PRODUCTION OF SCALE: AN UNFINISHED PROJECT

As Tsing (2012, 145) puts it, scale is fundamentally concerned with 'the relationship between the small and the large'. But McCarthy has noted the 'threatening unmanageability of scale as a concept', as well as the word's 'slipperiness' (2006, 33, 25). It is 'a complex and highly abstract noun that expresses a number of different kinds of proportional relations' (McCarthy, 2006, 21). The word is sometimes used to refer simply to 'size' or, in its geographical use, 'spatial extent' (Marston, 2000, 220), but it also usually implies a graduated succession of steps or a structured series of levels. Crucially, scale 'is not simply an external fact awaiting discovery but a way of framing conceptions of reality' (Delaney & Leitner, 1997, 94–5). It is 'the spatial dimensionality necessary for a particular kind of view, whether up close or from a distance, microscopic or planetary' (Tsing, 2005, 58).

The 'recognition that what constitutes the regional, urban or the local is not contained within a particular physical territory' (Bulkeley, 2005, 884), and the broader acknowledgement that scale is actively *produced* and *practised*, still comes up against the common-sense use of scale as 'just a neutral frame for viewing the world' (Tsing, 2005, 58). Scales are often the elements kept stable in studies of other objects—not least, as we have seen, in studies of music. Smith (1992, 61) has criticised the 'trivializ[ation] of] geographical scale as merely a question of methodological preference for the researcher', suggesting that this trivialisation partly explains why 'the division of the world into localities, regions, nations, and so forth is essentially taken for granted' (ibid.; see also Latour, 2007; Jones III et al., 2017). Sets of nested and/or hierarchical scales tend to be 'assumed in advance', functioning as an a priori 'transcendent model' that makes it 'difficult to conceive the world otherwise' (Pyyhtinen, 2017, 301). It is in some sense surprising that these scalar categories have become so naturalised when they are by definition artificial abstractions: metaphorical frames used as tools for specific purposes. Tsing suggests that 'the ease with which our computers zoom across magnifications lulls us into the false belief that both knowledge and things exist by nature in precision-nested scales' (2012, 161; see also Latour, 2007). Édouard Glissant, in his *Treatise on the Whole-World*, highlights the religious basis of a scalar system that 'hold[s] together the generality of the Universal and the dignity of the human individual' (Glissant, 2020 [1997], 59). There is also surely also an explanation based in the rational, secular, scientific view of the world as subject to a set of inflexible and universal laws, the existence of which implies that the world's phenomena are more or less predictable and capable of being interpreted on a spectrum from the micro to the macro. I suggest that listening more carefully and critically to the scale of music can offer an additional explanation for how certain scalar concepts have been so successfully *scaled up*, in the process helping to challenge such 'false beliefs' and common-sense trivialisations of scale.

This denaturalisation project is important politically and intellectually. For example, the moment a researcher selects—perhaps out of necessity or at least convenience—from a prescribed menu of scales is a moment of drastic selectivity that will affect and frame the researcher's methods and findings (Marston et al., 2005). The implications for academic research are broader still: scale is implicated in conceptualisations of the relationship between the general and the specific, the universal and the particular, which affect perceptions about whether something is important or insignificant in relation, proportion or comparison to something else (see Tanoukhi, 2008; Brydon, 2016). As McCarthy explains: 'The kinds of relationships designated by *scale* go beyond the simple physical sense of size. They straddle the qualitative/quantitative divide, enabling conceptual movement between argument and evidence, generality and specificity, concreteness and abstraction' (McCarthy, 2006, 25). Researchers such as the musicologist Anna Bull have been keen to go 'beyond the microsocial' and take account of 'wider' contexts and conditioning factors (Bull, 2019, 1), in part because this helps with the political purchase of their research. (Sub-)disciplines can also be divided and ranked according to scale (McCarthy, 2006): compare, for example, micro- and macroeconomics, or local and global history. Crucially, academics can use scale in a way that gives it 'causal force' (Marston et al., 2005, 6). The 'global', for example, is often presented as unavoidable, 'neutralizing the agency of the local' (ibid.). Even dichotomies between, say, 'local resistance and global structures of capitalism' are unhelpful because, as Tsing explains, such binaries 'draw us into an imagery in which the global is homogeneous precisely because we oppose it to the heterogeneity we identify as locality. By letting the global appear homogeneous, we open the door to its predictability and evolutionary status as the latest stage in macronarratives' (Tsing, 2005, 58).

Scale is political because it concerns power. When scales are given a different hierarchical order, or even when a new scalar category is successfully introduced, these 'scale redefinitions alter and express changes in the geometry of power by strengthening power and control by some while disempowering others' (Swyngedouw, 1997, 169). Newstead et al. (2003, 486) assert that this is 'what scale in fact is: the temporary fixing of the territorial scope of particular modalities of power'. The fact that scalar fixes are produced and negotiated rather than natural and ontological does not mean that they do not exist, or that they merely describe the world (see Blakey, 2021). Scale's framing function gives it the power to make a difference. For Marston: 'the outcomes of these framings—the particular ways in which scale is constructed—are tangible and have material consequences' (2000, 221). For Smith, too: 'Scale is an active progenitor of specific social processes' (Smith, 1992, 66). He conceives it as 'the criterion of difference not between places so much as between different kinds of places' (1992, 64) and thus a key process of spatial differentiation.

For those working with an awareness of scaling's political power, then, it has been important 'to understand the origins, determination and inner coherence and differentiation of each scale as already contained within the structure of capital' (Jones III et al., 2017, 181). This has involved asking: 'What is it—what processes, what sorts of activities—that not only produces and demarcates relatively stable scales, but binds them together in some sort of a "nested hierarchy"?' (Mitchell, 2002, 71). And it has involved investigating what makes certain political scalar fixes work or what has made them appealing. Tsing has noted the tremendous effort involved in constructing and advocating for particular scalar systems, emphasising how the appeal of twenty-first-century globalism comes through its rhetorical and ideological association with progress, 'futurism', 'newness' and all-encompassing 'circulation' as opposed to 'imagined stagnant locals' (Tsing, 2000, 346). Much work in this field has been based on Smith's initial (2010 [1984]) work on 'uneven development' and capitalism's role in ordering space into a complex multi-scale system in which not all scales are equal. Smith argued that the conceptualisation and organisation of the landscape into regions, cities and nations of varying power was a capitalist scalar fix, and that the 'flow' and 'spacelessness' of capitalist globalism represented 'not the extinction of place per se but *the reinvention of place at a different scale*' (1996, 72; italics in original).

Smith's early economistic formulations of scale theory have been criticised for their 'rigidity and functionalism' (Jones III et al., 2017, 142), but he and others inspired by his theorising steadily developed a richer and more sophisticated set of analytical tools for studying the political and social dynamics of scale-making. A key contribution of this work has been the understanding that scales are rarely discretely organised; rather, they 'interpenetrate' (Marston, 2000, 227), as 'Links among scale-making projects can bring each project vitality and power' (Tsing, 2005, 58). Certain concepts of the regional and the national work to produce the global, for example, and a particular form of urbanisation is intrinsic to what we understand as globalisation. And Smith himself turned to analysis of a *cultural* production—an art piece named the 'Homeless Vehicle'—to demonstrate precisely this 'active social and political connectedness of apparently different scales, [and] their deliberate confusion and abrogation' (Smith, 1992, 66).

Smith's series of studies on conceptual artworks still represent some of the most direct attempts to appreciate the role of culture in scale-making, although there is room for a considerably deeper analysis of this process. Smith focused on art pieces—such as Krzysztof Wodiczko's 'Poliscar' and 'Homeless Vehicle'—that functioned simultaneously as 'an art object and a resolutely practical vehicle of urban reconquest' (Smith, 1996, 63). He wrote that the 'Homeless Vehicle' was an 'instrument of political empowerment' because it worked 'symbolically and practically', with an emphasis on the practical (Smith, 1992, 60). It practically enabled 'evicted people to "jump scales"—to organize the production and reproduction of daily life and to resist oppression and exploitation at a higher scale—over a wider geographical field' (ibid.). He emphasised the 'symbiosis of the functional and symbolic object', suggesting that this art piece 'works as critical art only to the extent that it is simultaneously functional' (ibid., 54). He had little to say about the scalar potential of artistic pieces and practices lacking an explicitly practical or functional dimension, however. This focus on the literal rather than the artistic, or the material over the representation, is characteristic of much work that builds upon Smith's studies of art objects. Newstead et al. (2003), for example, have also sought to apply Marxist and Smith-informed conceptions of scale-making to 'an arena of examination addressed by cultural geography—the production and contestation of cultural landscapes' and 'cultural identity' (Newstead et al., 2003, 485). Their attention to 'visions' and 'reimaginations' of scale focuses primarily on the branding and propaganda of political organisations and institutions, although they do analyse one art piece: the retablo of Braulio Barrientos. This work is interpreted as a representation of 'the counter-hegemonic' construction of scale (ibid., 487), building on Don Mitchell's point about 'the subversive power of labor mobility' for controlling scale (2002, 64; see also Herod, 2010). In Newstead et al.'s analysis, however, the scale-making significance of the artwork seems to come through what it depicts, namely Mexican migrants' border-transgressing creation of a transnational space. It is the artist's subjects more than the art form or artistic processes per se that are doing the scalar work in this account.

The opposite is true for Richard Howitt's work on the relationship between music and geographical scale. Howitt has taken the 'serendipitous homonym for both geographical and musical scales [as] a starting point' (Howitt, 1998, 50). (One of scale's many meanings derives from the Middle English word for ladder, and it was in this sense of 'climbing' that the word came to be applied in terms of musical scale [McCarthy, 2006, 22].) Howitt treats musical scales merely as 'a useful metaphor for understanding the ways in which geographical scale involves relations between elements of complex and dynamic geographical totalities' (Howitt, 1998, 49). Foregoing 'detailed musicological discussion' in favour of exploring musical scales as 'a metaphor of geographical scale' (ibid., 57), Howitt offers a different conceptualisation of scale—focusing on relations instead of just size or level—rather than an explanation of how scale is produced or contested, whether musically or otherwise. On the contrary, Howitt's conclusion calls for geographical scale to be treated as a relatively stable causal factor. But there is potential to develop work on music and scale beyond the 'serenditipitous homonym' and the merely metaphorical.

With the various musical examples that follow, I seek to go beyond Smith's and Howitt's work to emphasise not only how practice and metaphor are interconnected when it comes to scalar musickings, but also that music has a scale-making or scale-contesting power as art and as a cultural practice. I am following the work of Diana Brydon (2016) who, through focusing on decolonial literature, has highlighted how artistic experimentation 'negotiates scale', not least through 'troubl[ing] the prevailing paradigms and scales' and enabling the imagination of alternative scalar forms and relations (Brydon, 2016, 31; 28). I argue, in particular, that focusing on music allows the cultural production of scale to be more fully understood. To do so, I proceed through four examples of musical scale-making. With the examples I choose I make clear that I do not approach music as a set of completed 'works'. I am making sense of music in the context in which it is heard, focusing on listeners' diverse responses to and uses of the music. I am interested in all the cultural practices of music's 'being and doing' (Wood et al., 2007, 868), following Dorr's (2018) capacious approach to music that takes in performance, listening and other aspects of 'musicking' (Small, 1998). The book does, however, include some more-or-less 'formal' musical analysis because specific compositional features, performance techniques and arrangements are part of the range of methods through which musicians might effect the cultural production of scale.

First, I analyse the experimental scalar agility and dexterity of Janelle Monáe, an American musician whose output spans the genres of R&B, psychedelic soul, hip-hop and funk. Focusing on her series of 'Metropolis' concept records, I explore Monáe's musical creation of a multi-scalar world, highlighting the range of simple and complex musical techniques through which she produces scalar multiplicity and interrelations. I argue that the scalar qualities of this world—and her ability to explore different relationships between different scales of social life, from the body to the metropolitan to the universal—make her music politically transgressive.

Second, I analyse the 'grime' genre's conjuring and use of the postcode scale—a form of what is often referred to as 'intense' or 'hyper' localism—as an example of the political deployment of scale as 'level of resolution'. Building on the work of Dan Hancox (2013, 2018), Monique Charles (2016, 2019), Joy White (2019, 2020) and others, and showing how grime differs from other rap-based genres and scenes that also use local lyrical references, the chapter uses examples from the music of Wiley, Roll Deep, Dizzee Rascal and Nadia Rose to explore how the genre's distinctive repetition, rhythmic intensification, staccato rapping style and selective musical audience-building contribute to a modernist, fine-grained postcode scale that has been used in political protests contesting the meaning of the 'local'.

Third, Louis Armstrong's 'What a Wonderful World' is highlighted to exemplify popular music's tendency and ability to build from the particular into the general—or to connect the personal to the universal. I explore how the musical transition to what Glissant calls 'Whole-World thinking' functions in various cover versions of the song, including politically charged live performances at a Swedish climate protest in 2019, and outside Lviv train station (and widely shared on social media) during Russia's ongoing invasion of Ukraine. I focus on how the song's crucial 'tritone substitution' chord—which is what musically accompanies the lyrics' logical leap from local observation to universal claim—is performed differently in different contexts, and I highlight how its inter-scalar element is crucial to its functioning both as a ubiquitous popular song and, in specific contexts, as a protest song.

Drawing on Grant Olwage's (2004) accounts of 'musical colonialism', and especially Kofi Agawu's (2016) work on 'tonality as a colonizing force', the fourth chapter explores music's colonial processes as a musical 'scale-making project' and an effort to produce a certain sonic 'scalability' (following Tsing, 2005, 2012). I draw attention to the role of music in the expansion of European mission stations and colonial settlements in southern Africa in the early decades of the nineteenth century, before the periods that Agawu and Olwage focus on. I do so by focusing on the scale-building project of missionary music scholars in London, and I show how this process was connected to contemporary debates about slavery, empire, race and humanity.

With these four examples—focusing on an artist, a genre, a (section of a) song, and an international musical-colonial policy—the book demonstrates the richness of music's scalar relations, highlighting how diverse practices of musicking in varied genres, in different historical and political contexts, and among different musical communities, can contribute to the cultural production of scale. The final concluding chapter highlights how, while music can be understood in relation to 'large-scale' geopolitical processes such as colonialism, it also provides a means of contesting dominant scalar systems and hierarchies, and of imagining and inaugurating a world scaled otherwise.

REFERENCES

Agawu, K. (2016). Tonality as a colonizing force in Africa. In R. Radano & T. Olaniyan (Eds.), *Audible empire: Music, global politics, critique* (pp. 334–355). Duke University Press.

Bennett, A., & Peterson, R. A. (Eds.). (2004). *Music scenes: Local, translocal and virtual*. Vanderbilt University Press.

Blakey, J. (2021). The politics of scale through Rancière. *Progress in Human Geography, 45*(4), 623–640.

Brown, A., O'Connor, J., & Cohen, S. (2000). Local music policies within a global music industry: Cultural quarters in Manchester and Sheffield. *Geoforum, 31*(4), 437–451.

Brydon, D. (2016). Experimental writing and reading across borders in decolonizing contexts. *Ariel: A Review of International English Literature, 47*(1), 27–58.

Bulkeley, H. (2005). Reconfiguring environmental governance: Towards a politics of scales and networks. *Political Geography, 24*(8), 875–902.

Bull, A. (2019). *Class, control, and classical music*. Oxford University Press.

Charles, M. (2016). Grime central!: Subterranean ground-in grit engulfing manicured mainstream spaces. In K. Andrews (Ed.), *Blackness in Britain* (pp. 89–100). Routledge.

Charles, M. (2019). Grime and spirit: On a hype! *Open Cultural Studies, 3*(1), 107–125.

Connell, J., & Gibson, C. (2003). *Sound tracks: Popular music, identity, and place*. Routledge.

Delaney, D., & Leitner, H. (1997). The political construction of scale. *Political Geography, 16*(2), 93–97.

Diamond, B. (2007). 'Allowing the listener to fly as they want to': Sámi perspectives on indigenous CD production in northern Europe. *The World of Music*, 23–48.

Dorr, K. A. (2018). On Site. In *Sound: Performance geographies in América Latina*. Duke University Press.

Duffy, M. (2017). Listening assemblages: Re-sounding place and mapping the affects of sound. In P. Moisala et al. (Eds.), *Musical encounters with Deleuze and Guattari* (pp. 189–203). Bloomsbury.

Dunbar-Hall, P., & Gibson, C. (2000). Singing about nations within nations: Geopolitics and identity in Australian indigenous rock music. *Popular Music & Society, 24*(2), 45–73.

Dunn, K. (2016). *Global punk: Resistance and rebellion in everyday life*. Bloomsbury Publishing.

Feld, S. (2000). A sweet lullaby for world music. *Public Culture, 12*(1), 145–171.

Fraser, A. (2010). The craft of scalar practices. *Environment and Planning A, 42*(2), 332–346.

Futrell, R., Simi, P., & Gottschalk, S. (2006). Understanding music in movements: The white power music scene. *The Sociological Quarterly, 47*(2), 275–304.

Glissant, É. (2020). *Treatise on the whole-world* (C. Britton, Trans.). Liverpool University Press.

Groth, S. K. (2020). 'Diam!' (be quiet!): Noisy sound art from the global south. In S. K. Groth & H. Schulze (Eds.), *The Bloomsbury handbook of sound art* (pp. 107–120). Bloomsbury.

Guilbault, J. (1993). On redefining the 'local' through world music. *The World of Music, 35*(2), 33–47.

Hamelink, W. (2016). *The sung home: Narrative, morality, and the Kurdish nation.* Brill.

Hancox, D. (2013). *Stand up tall: Dizzee rascal and the birth of grime.* Kindle Editions.

Hancox, D. (2018). *Inner city pressure: The story of grime.* HarperCollins.

Harris, K. (2000). 'Roots'?: The relationship between the global and the local within the extreme metal scene. *Popular Music, 19*(1), 13–30.

Herod, A. (2010). *Scale.* Routledge.

Howitt, R. (1998). Scale as relation: Musical metaphors of geographical scale. *Area, 30*(1), 49–58.

Jones, J. P., III, Leitner, H., Marston, S. A., & Sheppard, E. (2017). Neil Smith's scale. *Antipode, 49*, 138–152.

Kong, L. (1995). Popular music in geographical analyses. *Progress in Human Geography, 19*(2), 183–198.

Kong, L. (1996). Popular music in Singapore: Exploring local cultures, global resources, and regional identities. *Environment and Planning D: Society and Space, 14*(3), 273–292.

Kong, L. (1997). Popular music in a transnational world: The construction of local identities in Singapore. *Asia Pacific Viewpoint, 38*(1), 19–36.

Kruse, H. (2010). Local identity and independent music scenes, online and off. *Popular Music and Society, 33*(5), 625–639.

Latour, B. (2007). *Reassembling the social: An introduction to actor-network-theory.* Oxford University Press.

Lena, J. C. (2012). *Banding together: How communities create genres in popular music.* Princeton University Press.

Lerdahl, F. (1988). Tonal pitch space. *Music Perception, 5*(3), 315–349.

Makkonen, T. (2015). Northern comfort: Geographical scale, locality and the evolution of networks in the Finnish metal music genre. *Area, 47*(3), 334–340.

Marston, S. A. (2000). The social construction of scale. *Progress in Human Geography, 24*(2), 219–242.

Marston, S. A., Jones, J. P., III, & Woodward, K. (2005). Human geography without scale. *Transactions of the Institute of British Geographers, 30*(4), 416–432.

McCarthy, A. (2006). From the ordinary to the concrete: Cultural studies and the politics of scale. In M. White & J. Schwoch (Eds.), *Questions of method in cultural studies* (pp. 21–53). Blackwell.

Mitchell, D. (2002). Controlling space, controlling scale: Migratory labour, free speech, and regional development in the American West. *Journal of Historical Geography, 28*(1), 63–84.

Moisala, P., Leppänen, T., Tiainen, M., & Väätäinen, H. (2014). Noticing musical becomings: Deleuzian and Guattarian approaches to ethnographic studies of musicking. *Current Musicology, 98,* 71–93.

Morgan, M., & Bennett, D. (2011). Hip-hop & the global imprint of a black cultural form. *Daedalus, 140*(2), 176–196.

Newstead, C., Reid, C. K., & Sparke, M. (2003). The cultural geography of scale. In K. Anderson, M. Domosh, S. Pile, & N. Thrift (Eds.), *Handbook of cultural geography* (pp. 485–497). Sage.

O'Connor, A. (2002). Local scenes and dangerous crossroads: Punk and theories of cultural hybridity. *Popular Music, 21*(2), 225–236.

Olwage, G. (2004). Discipline and choralism: The birth of musical colonialism. In A. J. Randall (Ed.), *Music, power, and politics* (pp. 33–54). Routledge.

Omoniyi, T. (2006). Hip-hop through the world Englishes lens: A response to globalization. *World Englishes, 25*(2), 195–208.

Pyyhtinen, O. (2017). Matters of scale: Sociology in and for a complex world. *Canadian Review of Sociology/Revue canadienne de sociologie, 54*(3), 297–308.

Reuter, A. (2022a). Who let the DAWs out? The digital in a new generation of the digital audio workstation. *Popular Music and Society, 45*(2), 113–128.

Reuter, A. (2022b). Pop materialising: Layers and topological space in digital pop music. *Organised Sound, 27*(1), 59–68.

Saldanha, A. (2002). Music, space, identity: Geographies of youth culture in Bangalore. *Cultural Studies, 16*(3), 337–350.

Shelemay, K. K. (2011). Musical communities: Rethinking the collective in music. *Journal of the American Musicological Society, 64*(2), 349–390.

Small, C. (1998). *Musicking: The meanings of performing and listening.* Wesleyan University Press.

Smith, N. (1992). Contours of a spatialized politics: Homeless vehicles and the production of geographical scale. *Social Text, 33,* 55–81.

Smith, N. (1995). Remaking scale: Competition and cooperation in prenational and postnational Europe. In H. Eskelinen & F. Snickars (Eds.), *Competitive European peripheries* (pp. 59–74). Springer.

Smith, N. (1996). Spaces of vulnerability: The space of flows and the politics of scale. *Critique of Anthropology, 16*(1), 63–77.

Smith, N. (2010). *Uneven development: Nature, capital, and the production of space.* University of Georgia Press.

Straw, W. (1991). Systems of articulation, logics of change: Communities and scenes in popular music. *Cultural Studies, 5*(3), 368–388.

Swyngedouw, E. (1997). Excluding the other: The production of scale and scaled politics. In R. Lee & J. Wills (Eds.), *Geographies of economies* (pp. 167–176). Arnold.

Tanoukhi, N. (2008). The scale of world literature. *New Literary History, 39*(3), 599–617.

Taylor, J. (2012). *Playing it queer: Popular music, identity and queer world-making.* Peter Lang.

Tsing, A. L. (2000). The global situation. *Cultural Anthropology, 15*(3), 327–360.

Tsing, A. L. (2005). *Friction: An ethnography of global connection.* Princeton University Press.

Tsing, A. L. (2012). On nonscalability: The living world is not amenable to precision-nested scales. *Common Knowledge, 18*(3), 505–524.

Watson, A. (2008). Global music city: Knowledge and geographical proximity in London's recorded music industry. *Area, 40*(1), 12–23.

Westinen, E. (2014). *The discursive construction of authenticity: Resources, scales and polycentricity in Finnish hip hop culture.* PhD dissertation, University of Jyväskylä.

White, J. (2019). Growing up in 'the ends': Identity, place and belonging in an urban East London neighbourhood. In S. Habib & M. R. M. Ward (Eds.), *Identities, youth and belonging: International perspectives* (pp. 17–33). Routledge.

White, J. (2020). *Terraformed: Young black lives in the inner city.* Repeater.

Wood, N., Duffy, M., & Smith, S. J. (2007). The art of doing (geographies of) music. *Environment and Planning D: Society and Space, 25*(5), 867–889.

CHAPTER 2

Musical Metropolis: Janelle Monáe's Scalar Agility

Abstract Janelle Monáe—whose output spans the genres of R&B, psychedelic soul, hip-hop and Afrofuturist funk—is a prime example of a musician with scalar agility. Through a range of simple and complex musical techniques in a series of 'Metropolis' concept records, she has produced a multi-scalar 'sonic fiction'. The scalar qualities and relations of this musical world—and her ability to musically subvert, split and reimagine the relationships between scales such as the body, the metropolitan, the global and the universal in tracks such as 'Dance or Die' and 'Cold War'—make her work politically transgressive and capable of unsettling the present scaled reality.

Keywords Janelle Monáe • Scalecraft • Afrofuturism • Metropolis • Cold War • Sonic fiction

Listen to:
Janelle Monáe, 'Cold War' (2010)
Janelle Monáe, 'Dance or Die' (2010)

The Kansas City-born singer-songwriter, rapper, actor and producer Janelle Monáe attracts enthusiastic attention for her complex and innovative pop music. I suggest she is also a prime example of a musician with scalar agility: the ability to explore, through her music, a multi-scalar world, and to generate new and politically unsettling relationships between the different scales of social life. It is because of her musical style, and the scalar agility of her songwriting, that she is able to critique and affect the scales of the world. Her style—which incorporates sounds and features from R&B, psychedelic folk, musical theatre and hip-hop—has been called 'Afro-Sonic Feminist Funk' (Valnes, 2017), while Monáe describes her music as 'cybersoul'. For Hassler-Forest (2014, 11), Monáe's expansive, world-building musical oeuvre builds on '21st-century convergence culture and post-genre fantastic fiction'. Szaniawska (2019, 36) suggests Monáe works in the tradition and 'in the spirit of Black speculative fiction writers such as Octavia Butler, Nalo Hopkinson, Nnedi Okorafor, Tananarive Due and N.K. Jemisin who have imaged complex worlds', while Gipson (2016, 91) sees in Monáe 'the literary genius of Octavia Butler fused with the musical artistry of Prince'. The music media tends to list her eclectic influences—from Stevie Wonder to Salvador Dali to *Star Wars*—when trying to ascribe her to a genre, with one reviewer suggesting her output is 'about as bold as mainstream music gets, marrying the world-building possibilities of the concept album to the big tent genre-mutating pop of Michael Jackson and Prince in their prime' (Perpetua, 2010, n.p.). She attracts scholarly attention in part because she engages so boldly with popular culture and makes such dextrously political use of pop musical forms. Her music presents the 'visions and utopian ideas'—or the 'pluralistic, open-source blueprints'—required for social change (Aghoro, 2018, 339). Her work has a '"centrifugal" multiplicity of meaning' (Hassler-Forest, 2014, 6), and she makes use of numerous media forms—TV interviews, social media accounts, live performances, music videos and what she calls 'emotion pictures'—to augment and enrich her world-building. She has offered, within and against the restrictions of the twenty-first-century popular music industry, 'a musical, lyrical, visual, performative, and theoretical investigation into, and destabilization of, not only race and gender, but also sexuality, color, and class', demonstrating 'new liberatory possibilities created by African American cultural production' (English & Kim, 2013, 218). Through her creativity and dexterity she has developed 'a sound/sight corpus of black feminist knowledges that take advantage of social movement methods' (Redmond, 2011, 399; 406). She has also, I argue, demonstrated a dextrous 'scalecraft' (Fraser, 2010), producing differently scaled places through music, with critical attention to the relationships between such scaled categories as 'the global', the 'metro-politan' and 'the individual' or 'the body'.

Above all, Monáe is seen as 'creating alternative futures' (Valnes, 2017, 9) through a series of 'musical thought experiments' (Aghoro, 2018, 339) that draw on and reenergise the Afrofuturist tradition. In fact, with her 'futural sonic flare' (Gipson, 2016, 91) she has contributed a 'new, multi-valent … neo-Afrofuturism' (English & Kim, 2013). Afrofuturism, which first flourished in the 1960s, was driven by musicians who used new music technologies and techniques to create groove-driven 'sonic fictions' (Eshun, 1998). We can hear in Monáe's cybersoul the polyrhythmic com-plexity, 'timbral heterogeneity' and celebration of 'black vernacular intel-lectualism' associated with the big-band jazz and science-fiction-inspired funk (or 'astrofunk') of the early Afrofuturist musicians (Valnes, 2017, 3–4). Monáe has followed the likes of Sun Ra in constructing a space- and African-mythology-themed alternate universe in which she features as her rebel android alter-ego Cindi Mayweather (the 'Electric Lady'). Monáe's futuristic alternate universe—'Metropolis' (on which more below)—is a dystopian cityscape featuring a slave-like class of oppressed worker androids. Monáe's records and live performances feature sections of talk radio or other narrative to 'add world-building texture' that draws 'explicit parallels between the futuristic storyworld and contemporary social justice movements' (Hassler-Forest, 2016, 184). This is part of what Murchison (2018, 79) describes as Monáe's 'discursive practices and performative acts that push against the bounds and binds of existing social relations and power structures'. It is also part of 'her agency of worlding alternate spaces that intersect with the realm of the "real"' (Aghoro, 2018, 339). Marquita R. Smith (2019) emphasises that Monáe's world-building is hardly escap-ist: she produces 'art that inventively addresses the issues of its time' and her 'sonic and visual aesthetics' are linked to her activism with the Black Lives Matter movement (M. R. Smith, 2019, 44; 34). She sees a continu-ation between the WondaLand that is part of her imaginary world and the WondaLand Atlanta-based artist collective to which she belongs (Hassler-Forest, 2014), and the opening monologue in her 'Q.U.E.E.N' video refers to Monáe's 'musical weapons programme' and the 'freedom move-ments that WondaLand disguised as songs, emotion pictures and works of art'. It is her 'combination of art and activism' (Jones, 2018, 44)—or, I would argue, her activism through art—that gives her Afrofuturist musical creations political power. She 'fuses social and cultural movements' (Redmond, 2011, 395). She presents, according to Jones (2018, 43), 'a literal and figurative "Kansas City"'. She sculpts alternative worlds, and alternative world-subject relations, that have 'the potential to turn imaginative projections into lived experience' (Aghoro, 2018, 339), inaugurating new sets of relations in differently scaled worlds.

Scale is a vital and often overlooked aspect of fantastical world-building, including in studies of Monáe's work. It is through her scalar agility that Monáe 'strategically intermixes space with racial and sexual politics, black feminism, historical narratives, and class conflicts' (Gipson, 2016, 92). One scholar who has highlighted Monáe's scalar work is Shana Redmond (2011). Redmond notes Monáe's 'invention and use of scale' in the video for 'Cold War' (2011, 395), drawing on Katherine McKittrick's discussion of how cultural productions explore 'the place of black women in relation to various scales: in their minds, in their bodies, in their homes, in urban/rural centers, and in the nation' (McKittrick, 2000, 126). Redmond (2011, 394) also positions Monáe in a tradition of black women using their bodies creatively 'to critique and to resituate history'. Undoubtedly one of Monáe's main scalar contributions is to entirely unsettle the idea of 'the body' as a coherent, stable scale of social reality. Monáe's ArchAndroid/Cindy Mayweather/Electric Lady persona(s) necessitates a split in the category of the body, with different sets of relations for her android and human forms, albeit she has a 'thoroughly fluid relationship to her alter ego' which is 'inseparable from the "real" persona she performs as a twenty-first-century pop artist' (Hassler-Forest, 2016, 184; see also Szaniawska, 2019, 40). Through her androgynous dress and android persona—which is itself a kind of human-machine hybrid or 'organic-technological assemblage' (Aghoro, 2018, 339)—Monáe models a 'multiplicity of self' (Tembo, 2019, 197), inviting her audience 'to imagine a queer multiplicity of being' (Szaniawska, 2019, 40). Aside from the robot-with-human-flesh imagery she uses on her record covers, we also see her exploration of human-machine bodily hybridity in her stiff and frenzied dance gestures, her signature style of performing with widening, unblinking eyes, and, most notably, in her singing voice. She uses a technologically produced 'robotic' sound in her singing, such as on 'Mushrooms and Roses' (2010) in which she sings of 'lonely droids' and their romantic dreams featuring 'kisses and electricity'. Of course using a robotic voice sound is not new, nor is the 'robo-diva' persona (R. James, 2008). More distinctive, however, is Monáe's use of her un-technologically-mediated voice to create a robotic sound. She often sings in a machinic, expressionless and repetitive style, such as in the verses of 'Tightrope'

(2010) where she raps rhythmically, rarely varying from a single pitch, or in 'Electric Lady' (2013) where the introductory 'lec-le-le-lec-le-lec-le-lec-lec-tric—lay-le-le-lay-le-lay-le-lady' resembles a digital sample or robotic glitch. By embracing 'her role as the mediator … between androids and humans', Monáe 'foreground[s] the contingency of the human, particularly of the black female body' (English & Kim, 2013, 228; 218; see also Eshun, 1998). Monáe's music manifests 'the malleability of the very concept of "the human"' (Valnes, 2017, 1). Through various musical techniques she explores the idea of bodies in terms of what Blackman has described as 'bodies as assemblages of human and non-human processes … extending our concern with corporeality to species bodies, psychic bodies, machinic bodies and other-worldly bodies', questioning 'our expectations of clearly defined boundaries between the psychological, social, biological, ideological, economic and technical' (Blackman, 2012, 1; see also Cimini, 2016).

There are important political implications to this, especially when considered in terms of scale. As Szaniawska (2019, 40) points out, Monáe's work is concerned with 'Black women's exclusion from the category of the human'. Her music allows her 'audience to imagine a revolutionary potential that the Black female body could yield', especially the 'freedom to move … between different embodiments' (ibid.). This works as a political strategy because it recognises the messy, structured realities of the world and, crucially, different bodies' differential relationships to the scales of social life. Monáe's music explores the potential of individuals and bodies of different kinds, but it is not in the realm of pure potential and fluidity of identity. Monáe's Cindi Mayweather is a messianic figure, but it is significant that she is destined to lead the oppressed worker class of android Others. Monáe's world-building is based around intersectional inequalities and differential access to spaces of power. As Yates-Richard (2021, 39) puts it: Monáe does reference '"black bodies", but suggests that these bodies inhabit this future space-time differently'. Her musical explorations 'of black cyborg womanhood expose, critique and reimagine "modes of the human", while also refusing notions of virtual disembodiment as freedom' (Yates-Richard, 2021, 47).

This is particularly clear when Monáe's music explores the relationships between scales. An interesting song to analyse in this light is 'Cold War', the second single from her debut album The ArchAndroid (2010). Redmond (2011) focuses especially on the 'Cold War' music video to 'highlight the ways that Monáe plays with scale to adjust the relationship between body and mind, and between history and lived experience', inserting herself 'into Cold War historiography as she performs an alternative geography that produces space and its meaning through her own sexualized and racialized body' (Redmond, 2011, 405–6). Redmond emphasises 'Monáe's invention and use of scale', suggesting that the 'Cold War' historical framework enables Monáe to explore how 'state powers continue to employ scale to enact competing world visions' (Redmond, 2011, 395). Much of Redmond's analysis relates to the juxtaposition between global-historical lyrical themes and the music video's intimate focus on Monáe's disrobed body, but there is more to be said about how 'Cold War' musically explores the relationship between the individual and global scales. As Gipson (2016, 100) points out, 'Cold War' is an 'intensely personal' song. But it is a strange kind of 'personal' song in the sense that Monáe uses few of the musical techniques or features that are commonly used to convey personal intimacy or depth of emotion. There is a largely steady, fast-paced rock beat, and instrumentation that sounds 'flat' and almost distant. What is remarkable is how little complexity or detail can be heard in the accompaniment, especially in comparison with the rhythmic and melodic variety of her other tracks. The synthesised chords are steady with no rhythmic variation. There is also very little space, and Monáe never uses the techniques of close-to-the-microphone vocal recording that are conventionally used to generate a sense of emotional intimacy (see Kraugerud, 2021). Instead, she sings—at least during the verses and chorus—at a stable, high volume, almost battling to be heard over the backing instrumentation. All of this contributes to her expression of the relationship between the individual and the global or perhaps more properly the inter- or transnational 'large-scale' context, of which the Cold War is a lyrical metaphor. We see this too in the juxtaposition between the grand-scale lyrical content of the bridge section, which sounds almost like a saga or sermon ('May all evil stumble as it flies in the world/All the tribes come and the mighty will crumble'), and the more personal verse that follows: 'I'm trying to find my peace/I was made to believe there's something wrong with me/And it hurts my heart'. This line—'I was made to believe there's something wrong with me'—functions as the emotional and musical climax of the song (which has a rather unconventional ending, as a key change leads not, per convention, to a more triumphant repetition of the chorus but instead to an immediate fade to close). The phrasing—being 'made to believe'—implies impersonal forces acting upon the individual, causing pain, and reinforces the wider message of the song, which is about how people can be made to live in a state of vigilance in a context of con-stant implied threat. The unemotiveness that Monáe uses here—and else-where in her oeuvre (see, e.g., Valnes, 2017), often represented by the robotic singing style and persona described above—functions in 'Cold War' as a political critique of an individual-world relationship that forces people into vigilance and defensiveness. Monáe's exploration of this individual-world relationship should also be understood in relation to the more positive kind of 'universal' musical space she creates in other songs. In 'What An Experience' (2013, in which she sings of how 'the world's just made to fade') and 'Say You'll Go' (2010, in which she references Nirvana, Samsara, Dhammapada and Noah's Ark), for example, she sings about the purity and spirituality of love in a kind of abstract, placeless space characterised by musical simplicity and a subtle or non-existent rhythm section. Here, a positive universality, a scale beyond the social, equates essentially to abstract placelessness and contextless, while 'Cold War' has a more cynical or critical take on the relationship between people and their wider socio-political reality.

In Monáe's musical world-building, the individual-context relationship varies, including within a set scale. It is notable that Monáe's musical world is on the urban or metropolitan scale, organised around a science-fictional 'Metropolis' (although arguably the conventional 'urban' cate-gory does not fit Monáe's Metropolis). 'Metropolis' is the name she gives to her four-part series of concept records that explore this world domi-nated by a metropolis. The album cover of 2010s *The ArchAndroid*, which contains suites II and III of the 'Metropolis' series, features Monáe wear-ing a cityscape headdress that is clearly inspired by Fritz Lang's classic science-fiction movie *Metropolis* (1927), which depicts class conflict in a futuristic urban dystopia. In Monáe's world, Metropolis is the last remain-ing city on earth. She is committed to the idea of the metropolis—with its imperial connotations of a powerful city acting at a distance on other places—as a terrain of political struggle. She does not see it as an inher-ently dominating concept; rather, she wants to save and transform it, and her 'Metropolis' series of musical productions are committed to exploring cultural-political struggle at the metropolitan scale. Crucially, however, Monáe produces the metropolitan as a key scale of political contestation by representing it not as a single, stable category but as heterogeneous, with different kinds of spaces within it, where struggles over it take place. For example, Monáe depicts Metropolis as a source of threat in 'Dance or Die' (2010). This sense of threat or watchful tension in an urban setting emerges as the song begins with a low, minimal bass-line and quiet, spare percussion from a conga drum, with occasional synthesised noises that evoke passing traffic. When Monáe's vocals first come in—rapping about 'running for your life' and how 'war is in the streets'—they are recorded in a low whisper, close to the microphone, as if she fears being overheard. After the multi-voiced chorus comes in to establish the premise that the Metropolitan dwellers are awaiting 'the one' (i.e. Monáe's android-saviour alter-ego Cindi Mayweather), Monáe's rapping becomes louder, higher-pitched, more confident, and the relationship of threat between the singer and the metropolitan space is reversed by the end of the song.

Monáe's listeners also come to understand Metropolis as comprised of different kinds of spaces. She refers to both 'the kingdom' and 'the nation' in 'Dance or Die', and describes the strength and transgressive power of a 'Ghetto Woman' (2013). There are also collective spaces of live perfor-mance within Metropolis, and this is where she presents and explores radi-cal, countercultural political potential. 'Tightrope', for example, establishes this kind of space through occasional addresses to an imagined audience (e.g. 'ladies and gentlemen, [introducing] the funkiest horn section in Metropolis!'), and through a rapped dialogue between Monáe and her collaborator Big Boi that also features extensive backing vocals, including call-and-response with a choir. Her first vocalisation is a loud, high-pitched 'wow!', introducing herself more radically and boldly than in 'Dance or Die'. Indeed, 'Tightrope' is musically unruly, with different sections and breakdowns in which different instruments come to the fore. Unlike in 'Cold War', 'Tightrope' features funk-style syncopated rhythms and com-plex instrumentation to establish this sense of collectivity and the radical potential that comes with it. Here is a space of live musical performance *within* Metropolis that is also heard as a threat to how the metropolitan is defined.

All this is part of Monáe's scalar agility: her ability to produce a multi-scalar world through music, and to explore different relationships between different scales of social life. Her scaled musical productions enable analy-sis and critique of how different bodies have different kinds of experiences of, say, the urban or metropolitan scale, which is itself internally differenti-ated, emphasising too that hegemonic categories of social life can be chal-lenged and relationships between scales transformed. Even the city streets are presented not as a straightforwardly threatening space—rather, the relationship of threat changes musically. Her music explores a global or transnational geopolitical context that is presented in terms of its oppressive power in relation to the individual, but there is also a 'universal' space of emancipation. Monáe's 'scalecraft' is her ability to produce these complex scales and scalar relations in music. Sometimes she does this relatively simply, such as when the collective space of radical musical performance is produced through syncopation and complex rhythmic interplays plus unstructured backing vocals and more obvious features like addresses to an audience and crowd noise, or when the universal, abstract space is represented through musical simplicity and a lack of structure and rhythm. She also represents scalar relations through innovative, unconventional, complex musical choices to explore deeply personal and emotional themes, such as in Cold War. Fundamentally, Monáe's musical multiplicity of scale is her political strategy for producing new scalar relationships in the real world. It is the multiplicity of the body and of the metropolitan that is crucial, as well as the multiple relations to and between these scales. For Monáe, bodies are always already mediated and have different relationships to the spaces of social life. The relationship between the individual, the metropolitan and/or the global is not stable. This means these relationships are open to contestation and can be made anew, including through cultural practices. This is what makes scale a cultural-political question and a terrain for struggle. Monáe presents an Afrofuturist vision of a territory organised around a 'Metropolis', but the Metropolis is unstable, in question—and her music centres that question, showing where the tension and radical political potential lies. This is musical world-building, and that world has a scale, or rather complex scalar relations that Monáe explores musically. Monáe's musicking may also be seen as example of a kind of 'decolonizing literary experimentation', following Brydon (2016, 30), albeit with a musical rather than literary mode of exploring 'alternative scalar relations along with the vitality of nonscalable worlds' (ibid.). In particular, Monáe's music is involved in 'the production of non-nested modalities of scale' (Brydon, 2016, 31), with the Metropolitan neither neatly subordinate to the global or universal, nor equally accessible from a single 'individual' scale. The political potential of this—the connection between the musical world and the scales of social life—is realised also through the several connections Monáe makes as a pop musician between her cultural productions and the real world. In Monáe's 'literal and figurative "Kansas City"' (Jones, 2018, 43), music and other cultural productions and practices are the means of political transformation. Monáe's WondaLand Arts Society works with the same aims and methods in this musically produced world and in reality (English & Kim, 2013, 226), and she understands her futuristic 'sonic fictions' (Eshun, 1998) as capable of unsettling and resisting the present scaled reality.

REFERENCES

Aghoro, N. (2018). Agency in the afrofuturist ontologies of Erykah Badu and Janelle Monáe. *Open Cultural Studies, 2*(1), 330–340.

Blackman, L., 2012. *Immaterial Bodies: Affect, Embodiment, Mediation.* Sage.

Brydon, D. (2016). Experimental writing and reading across borders in decolonizing contexts. *Ariel: A Review of International English Literature, 47*(1), 27–58.

Cimini, A. (2016). Gilles Deleuze and the musical Spinoza. In B. Hulse & N. Nesbitt (Eds.), *Sounding the virtual: Gilles Deleuze and the theory and philosophy of music* (pp. 129–144). Routledge.

English, D. K., & Kim, A. (2013). Now we want our funk cut: Janelle Monáe's neo-Afrofuturism. *American Studies, 52*(4), 217–230.

Eshun, K. (1998). *More brilliant than the sun: Adventures in sonic fiction.* Quartet Books.

Fraser, A. (2010). The craft of scalar practices. *Environment and Planning A, 42*(2), 332–346.

Gipson, G. D. (2016). Afrofuturism's musical princess Janelle Monáe: Psychedelic soul message music infused with a sci-fi twist. In R. Anderson & C. E. Jones (Eds.), *Afrofuturism 2.0: The rise of Astro-blackness* (pp. 91–107). Lexington.

Hassler-Forest, D. (2014). The politics of world-building: Heteroglossia in Janelle Monáe's Afrofuturist WondaLand. *Para-doxa, 26,* 284–303.

Hassler-Forest, D. (2016). *Science fiction, fantasy, and politics: Transmedia world-building beyond capitalism.* Rowman & Littlefield.

James, R. (2008). 'Robo-Diva R&B': Aesthetics, politics, and black female robots in contemporary popular music. *Journal of Popular Music Studies, 20*(4), 402–423.

Jones, C. L. (2018). 'Tryna free Kansas City': The revolutions of Janelle Monáe as digital griot. *Frontiers: A Journal of Women Studies, 39*(1), 42–72.

Kraugerud, E. (2021). *Come closer: Acousmatic intimacy in popular music sound.* PhD dissertation, Department of Musicology, University of Oslo.

McKittrick, K. (2000). 'Black and 'Cause I'm Black I'm Blue: Transverse racial geographies in Toni Morrison's *The Bluest Eye. Gender, Place and Culture: A Journal of Feminist Geography, 7*(2), 125–142.

Murchison, G. (2018). Let's Flip it! Quare emancipations: Black queer traditions, Afrofuturisms, Janelle Monáe to Labelle. *Women and Music: A Journal of Gender and Culture, 22,* 79–90.

Perpetua, M. (2010). [Review:] The ArchAndroid, Janelle Monáe. *Pitchfork.* Accessed April 3, 2023, from https://pitchfork.com/reviews/albums/14271-the-archandroid/

Redmond, S. L. (2011). This safer space: Janelle Monáe's 'cold war'. *Journal of Popular Music Studies, 23*(4), 393–411.

Smith, M. R. (2019). Visions of Wondaland: On Janelle Monáe's Afrofuturistic vision. In S. Fast & C. Jennex (Eds.), *Popular music and the politics of hope: Queer and feminist interventions* (pp. 31–48). Routledge.

Szaniawska, A. (2019). Gestural refusals, embodied flights: Janelle Monáe's vision of black queer futurity. *The Black Scholar, 49*(4), 35–50.

Tembo, K. D. (2019). On the (un)becoming of Cindi Mayweather: The transhumanist gynoid performativity of Janelle Monáe. In M. G. Hill (Ed.), *Black bodies and transhuman realities: Scientifically modifying the black body in posthuman literature and culture* (pp. 193–208). Rowman and Littlefield.

Valnes, M. (2017). Janelle Monáe and Afro-sonic feminist funk. *Journal of Popular Music Studies, 29*(3), 1–12.

Yates-Richard, M. (2021). 'Hell you talmbout': Janelle Monáe's black cyberfeminist sonic aesthetics. *Feminist Review, 127*(1), 35–51.

CHAPTER 3

A Postcode-Scale Genre: Grime's Scale as 'Level of Resolution'

Abstract The popular electronic music genre known as grime is often referred to as intensely 'local', even 'hyperlocal'. Its 'postcode scale' is an example of the political deployment of scale, understood as level of resolution. Examples from Wiley, Roll Deep and Dizzee Rascal demonstrate how the genre's distinctive repetition, rhythmic intensification and staccato rapping style contribute to a modernist, fine-grained, high-resolution postcode scale. Analysis of Nadia Rose's 2017 track 'Skwod' shows that grime tracks also use musical techniques to build a selective, by-no-means-all-inclusive audience, drawing attention to the boundaries of belonging. Grime has also been involved in struggles over definitions of the local, such as when 'Skwod' was used by intersectional feminists in place-specific antifascist protests. Overall, the intensely local or postcode-scale aesthetics of grime music are part of a socio-political strategy that draws attention to mechanisms of inclusion and exclusion, potentially remaking the borders of 'the local' when the genre's political potential is heard by particular listeners.

Keywords Grime • Postcode • Wiley • Dizzee Rascal • Bow • E3 • Nadia Rose • Sisters Uncut • Croydon • Protest song

© The Author(s) 2023
P. Dodds, *Music and the Cultural Production of Scale*,
https://doi.org/10.1007/978-3-031-36283-5_3

Listen to:
Wiley, 'Bow E3' (2006)
Nadia Rose, 'Skwod' (2017)

The popular electronic music genre known as grime emerged in the early 2000s, produced largely by young, black, working-class men in London's council estates (Charles, 2019, 108). It was always a disruptive, hectic and 'unruly' genre (White, 2020, 250), featuring 'squelchy' deep bass, trebly computer game samples, fast-paced rapping, skittish high-hat rhythms and rapid syncopated breakbeats. Grime grew, in its early years, out of rap battles or 'sound clashes' that took place within and between different crews of performers, and this turn-taking, participatory, semi-competitive, do-it-yourself crew culture gave grime its 'lo-fi, gritty, raw, grimy and unrefined sound' (Charles, 2019, 107). Grime music is often described as darker, less polished, more urgent and less 'cool' than precedents and comparators such as UK garage and US hip-hop. As a genre it built upon London's existing reggae, dancehall and jungle scenes and, as Joy White has explained, grime 'pushed back the juggernaut that was US hip-hop and rap and replaced it, in London at least, with a black-English aesthetic' (White, 2020, 266). Despite initial suspicion from the national media and suppression by the London police, grime is said to have 'independently emerged as a force that now defines urban Britain' (Woods, 2020, 300).

One characteristic that grime shares with hip-hop is its emphasis on local urban geographies, although grime is distinguished by the intensity of its fine-grained, postcode-scale locality. For many influential hip-hop artists, the neighbourhood 'is enunciated in terms that elevate it as a primary site of significance' (Forman, 2002, xix). This local identification with a relatively narrowly defined home place—often using references to specific streets, intersections and US dial codes—was always a means for creating a 'self-produced communal history' (Rose, 1989, 43), part of 'poor young black people's need to have their territories acknowledged, recognised and celebrated' (Rose, 1994, 11). Murray Forman, in his influential study of hip-hop's 'cultural production of urban sites of significance', identifies rappers' lyrical construction of 'the extreme local' (Forman, 2002, xix; xvii), arguing that they draw on narrower spatial references than other American popular music genres. This 'extreme local' seems to come from lyrical specificity, that is, from rappers' tendency to name identifiable places that are geographically smaller than cities, regions or nations. Grime artists do this too, but their localism is more distinctive and more 'extreme', not just in terms of lyrical specificity but also in terms of the aesthetic intensity with which they render their 'local'. Indeed, to understand the construction and significance of the local scale in grime, it is necessary to look beyond the lyrical references to specific places. Other distinctive musical features of the genre are highlighted here, namely the fast-paced staccato rapping, the lack or selective use of echo or reverb, the repetition of distorted or chopped-up samples, and the song structures built around rhythmic intensification (often through increased rhyme frequency) rather than melodic or lyrical progression. These features of grime do not make it a genre that is *more local* than others, but they are part of why the genre is heard as distinctively, intensely local, and they are what produce the particular intensity and significance of the genre's local scale. They are also what has given grime the power to intervene in geographies at different scales, and even to contribute to a redefinition of the meaning of the 'local' as a category.

Studies of grime have already highlighted its 'intense localism' (Hancox, 2018, 151). It is called 'microscopically local' (ibid., 154), even 'hyperlocal' (M. James, 2020; White, 2019, 23), with lyrics that go into 'molecular detail' (Hancox, 2013, 175). White suggests grime artists' focus on 'the lived experience of a specific and particular place' allows them to 'assert black urban identities that are hyper localised' (White, 2020, 254). This intense/microscopic/hyper localism, as well as the fact it 'sounds like where it is from' (White, 2020, 250), is apparently essential and integral to the genre: a defining characteristic, and one of the reasons it is both so popular and so artistically innovative. For Dan Hancox (2018, 151), 'Grime's strength was always in its intense localism, more than its expression of universal truths'. Its localism may be explained by the fact that marginalised groups, such as working-class black people, are more likely to experience a 'lack of access to non-local scales of social experience' (McCarthy, 2006). Grime's practitioners have been in various ways 'excluded from grander national or civic identities' (ibid.; for this argument see also Bramwell, 2015, 126). Grime artists have tended to have the legitimacy of their belonging questioned. There was the infamous example of grime's most prominent star, Dizzee Rascal, being asked on a BBC news programme in 2008: 'do you feel yourself to be British?' (Dizzee Rascal was born and raised in Britain and his answer was: 'of course I'm British man!'). Certainly grime musicians were initially marginalised, practitioners of an 'outsider art' (Hancox, 2018, 183), seen as a threat by the media and the police, and restricted from being able to perform even in their home city let alone represent wider national civic identity. Famously grime grew in its early years from a pirate radio culture, with illegal stations broadcasting from residential tower blocks in East London, often with fairly restricted broadcast radiuses that may have affected the 'local' nature of the music being produced—although in reality many of these stations could be heard up to 40 miles away (DJ Target, 2018, 158). (DJ Target (ibid., 140) also relates an amusing story about how the radius in which a record could be released was determined by how far an old Fiat Punto could get across London on a hot summer's day.) Moreover, White points out that grime may have originated in pirate radio but 'it came of age in the YouTube era' (White, 2020, 251; see also White, 2017; M. James, 2020). Grime quickly reached a wide, even global audience through the internet and mobile technologies, influencing music cultures around the world, so the 'local' sound was not due to some merely technological restriction in the location of the audience. Its 'intense localism' was and is an artistic choice, culturally produced.

It is also important to acknowledge that grime is by no means narrowly 'local' in the sense of being limited to one social scale. Ruth Adams (2019) has argued convincingly that the grime scene entails expressions of multiscalar identities—individual, local, national and transnational—and that grime artists are skilled in representing London's multicultural and globalised dimensions as much as its particular local communities. White likewise describes how 'grime operates at a local level, as an outernational space, and as a global enterprise' (White, 2020, 268). Although grime songs may focus on specific roads or council estates, they might also take in large regions of London: BMD's 'North Weezy' and Southside Allstars' 'Southside Riddim' claim to represent the whole of Northwest and South London respectively, each with populations of hundreds of thousands or even millions of people. Artists such as Lethal Bizzle have released tracks about 'London' as a whole, while Kano has taken on wider urban and national geographies in his 2007 'London Town' album and his 2016 single 'This is England', among others. Moreover, grime is 'simultaneously hyperlocal and international' (White, 2019, 22), rooted in international live music destinations such as Ayia Napa, and with strong influences from Black Atlantic traditions. Dizzee Rascal, once an outsider, quickly won national awards and performed at the opening ceremony of the London Olympics in 2012, at which he sported an 'E3' jacket referencing his home postcode in East London. Dizzee Rascal is now a global star although his latest album, 'E3 AF' from 2020, still insists on that local identification. It is through the local specificity that Dizzee gained national and global fame, and newer artists such as Stormzy (who identifies strongly with his home estate in South London) have achieved similar large-scale success. DJ Target suggests Dizzee Rascal was able to appeal not just to people who lived precisely where he lived, but also 'to kids all across the country living in similar circumstances' (DJ Target, 2018, 114). According to Hancox, Dizzee's identification with 'ghetto wherever' allowed him to speak to 'the urban margins across the world' (Hancox, 2018, 162). As Monique Charles puts it, grime's 'local specificity … create[s] spaces for national and international dialogue' (Charles, 2016, 1). Grime now has a worldwide audience *because* of its intense localism, and there are versions of it and genres inspired by it in other cities and countries.

The point, again, is that grime music is not inherently *more local* than many other kinds of music. The E3 postcode area mentioned by grime artists is a much larger spatial unit than the Chelsea Hotel sung about by several artists over several decades, or than Ed Sheeran's bedroom or the all-you-can-eat diner he references in 'Shape of You'. The E3 zone is also among the most densely populated areas of the UK. Even the Roman Road that features regularly in grime tracks is both larger and more popu-lous than the Beatles' 'Penny Lane'. One reason that grime is commonly understood to be intensely/microscopically/hyper local may be because 'gritty' urban estates and street corners are commonly understood to be 'more local' than other kinds of places, or less generally representative of—even exceptions to—larger-scale social units such as nations (for a criticism of this tendency, see Mitchell, 2002, 71). But while grime's focus is not necessarily 'smaller' or less civically/nationally/internationally sig-nificant than the spatial focus of other genres, grime artists do take a dif-ferent artistic approach to rendering place, using aesthetic techniques for a specific purpose, and with specific political intentions and implications. It is not an inherently 'more local' music that results naturally from its practitioners living 'more local' lives. The distinctively and intensely local scale of grime music is a cultural production.

Grime's local scale, which may be seen as a socio-political strategy, must be understood as a response to, and an intervention in, its socio-political context. Grime emerged initially from some of the poorest areas of the UK. Moreover, these East London boroughs and wards with high rates of poverty and deprivation sit side by side with the city's 'visible locations of great wealth' (White, 2020, 250). The skyscrapers of the City of London's

financial district dominate the view to the west, while Canary Wharf, home
to the headquarters of numerous multinational corporations, is even closer
to the south. The Tower Hamlets estate setting for Roll Deep's 2005
'When I'm 'Ere' video, for example, is just ten minutes' walk from the
towers of Credit Suisse, HSBC and One Canada Square. Dizzee Rascal
wrote most of his debut album 'Boy in Da Corner' while still at Langdon
Park School in Poplar, which was barely a kilometre from One Canada
Square. In a 2010 BBC London radio interview, Dizzee Rascal chose One
Canada Square as his favourite building, explaining: 'I could see it from all
angles as a kid. That was the highest building I could see from my bedroom … I remember when we were little, we had a conspiracy—we
thought that thing on the top of it was like aliens, and they were about to
fly off—loads of little theories like that' (quoted in Hancox, 2013, 175).
This has always been, as White (2020, 250) puts it, 'the backdrop to
grime': 'rich and poor communities that exist side by side but barely
touching. In these alien spaces, with bounded territories that are border
patrolled by private security, young people are living in proximity to these
heavily guarded structures of wealth and privilege—in plain sight, but
almost always out of reach' (ibid., 267; see also Charles, 2016, 93).
Grime's practitioners 'were exposed to (yet excluded from) fast social
change, i.e. gentrification, in the areas they lived' (Charles, 2019, 108).
For this reason, researchers have used the language of 'marginality' to
describe the socio-economic context of the grime scene (e.g. Charles,
2016, 89; White, 2019, 17; Charles, 2019, 124). For Orlando Woods,
grime emerged 'from the spatial margins of inner city London' and its
political aim has been 'to overcome the socio-spatial marginalization of
urban Britain' (Woods, 2020, 304; 295). Marginalisation may describe
the East London grime scene's relationship to an East London global elite
who are able to move more freely, unpoliced, but its connotation of spatial
peripheries is less appropriate. Rather, grime's practitioners may more
accurately be said to come from *overlooked* spaces and *contested* edges.
These spaces are relatively central, densely populated, close to some of
London's most iconic leisure, tourism and global capital sites, and yet not
seen, not included in an urban overview, not part of the city's or the
nation's story, not part of 'global' progress, and 'rendered out of time and
out of place' (White, 2019, 26). The kind of 'uneven development' and
urban inequality experienced by grime's listeners and practitioners is
exactly the political-economic basis, as Neil Smith (2010) sees it, of the
scalar system and spatial functioning of capitalism.

This is where grime's postcode scale comes in, with scale understood here to mean not just size or spatial extent but 'the level of resolution' (Marston, 2000, 220). Indeed, when something is 'small-scale' this usually entails finer-grained, high-resolution detail, alongside different selection criteria for the features included or excluded. For grime, greater granularity is a political strategy: its high level of resolution ensures a set of social realities come to the fore that may be absent from other music, even other popular music with an urban focus and scale. Grime's scale enables closer attention to the city's unevenness: to the stuff that falls in-between and to the detail that might otherwise be missed. It draws out the grime, or as Charles (2016) puts it, the 'subterranean ground-in grit engulfing manicured mainstream spaces'. And although the grime scene has collectively mapped London in high-resolution detail, each grime artist's emphasis and scale is based around what Richard Bramwell (2015, 125) calls 'a far more restricted political identity: the postcode'. The genre's 'postcode particularism' (ibid., 126) is expressed in part through the repeated references to postcodes in grime lyrics. Southside Allstars shout out basically every South London postcode, with different emcees representing SE1, SE5, SW11, SW18 and so on. Grime musicians in other UK cities such as Liverpool also use postcodes when making spatial references (Cohen, 2012). Skepta raps on 'Man' (2016), 'You know the postcode when you're talkin' road, better know that I speak that fluently'. Of course, Skepta also explains on 'That's Not Me' (2016): 'I don't really care about your postcode'. The postcode references should not be taken overly literally, as the British right-wing media does when it invokes grime in discussions of so-called 'postcode wars' between London gangs. Rather, the postcode symbolises the kind of 'hyperlocal demarcation' (White, 2020) that the music is exploring. It is an indication of grime's level of resolution.

The postcode is an appropriate choice for two main reasons. First, it fits in with grime's modernist self-styling. In music videos and other promotional imagery, artists such as Skepta and Dizzee Rascal are often framed by 1960s Brutalist tower blocks and council estates that were built around the same time that the UK's postcode system was introduced. Balfron Tower, for example, which features in Dizzee's and Wiley's self-branding, was built between 1965 and 1967 by the Labour-controlled Greater London Council, just as the famous left-wing Labour politician Tony Benn, as Postmaster General, announced the national application of postcodes. The first postcode was tested in Croydon, South London, where a proud grime scene includes Stormzy, Plastician and Nadia Rose. The use of postcodes therefore signals a distinctly, perhaps even coldly modern method of differentiating and organising space, foregoing what *essentially* differentiates places and instead fitting them into a modernist system. Rather than using the historic names for London's parishes and former villages, with their historic connotations, grime artists instead use the codes designed for municipal organisation in the second half of the twentieth century. For example, rather than naming 'Brockley', the etymology of which refers to 'a woodland clearing where badgers are seen', a grime MC can claim to represent 'SE4', which places them on an abstract, featureless spatial grid—albeit an off-kilter grid with a scale that does not apply evenly over all space, as the spatial extent of a postcode differs according to the characteristics of the place. This contributes to what Hancox describes as grime's 'sonic futurism': its 'sheer alien newness' produced by its video games samples, its 'off-kilter arrangements … dehumanised synths and cyborg basslines' (Hancox, 2018, 70). Using postcodes to designate places complements grime's 'sonic representation of the alien spaces that its creators occupy' (White, 2020, 250).

The second reason for this adoption of the postcode-scale is that it signifies granularity and high-resolution detail, at least in urban areas.[1] The postcode is the lowest level of aggregation used in national statistical gathering and municipal administration. Each of the UK's 121 postcode areas (such as 'SE13') is broken down into smaller units (such as 'SE13 6JL') that often cover just a few buildings—usually around 15 properties and no more than 100 'deliverable endpoints' or residences. This means a full postcode can cover an extremely small area of a densely populated city, perhaps even a few square metres. And although the spatial references grime artists use are actually the postcode areas rather than full postcodes—and therefore they are not *that* local in their spatial references— the postcode system nevertheless implies an organisation of space that is capable of greater geographical specificity, detail and granularity, and simultaneously malleable and variable according to how the space is

---

[1] In this postcode scale, not all space is equivalent or rendered at the same level of resolution. E3, with its high population density, is one of the smallest postcode areas in spatial terms, covering around six square kilometres. IV27 in northwest Scotland, by contrast, accounts for more than 2000 square kilometres. Maps of these two areas, produced at the postcode scale, would either have to show different features or be vastly different sizes.

inhabited. In densely populated areas, the postcode promises a higher level of resolution than the historic place name it replaces.

What makes grime intensely/microscopically/hyper local, however, is not its lyrical references to postcodes per se but more generally the way it renders its postcode scale musically. The intensity of grime tracks can make the local, at the postcode scale, seem claustrophobic and inescapable. A good example is Wiley's track 'Bow E3' from 2006, which presents E3 as of fundamental and undeniable social significance. (Wiley is now a renowned antisemite and conspiracy theorist, and his music and its politics have of course been reassessed, but his influence on the early development of the genre is still worth analysing.) Wiley raps over an instrumental constructed from a high-hat-and-snare beat, grime's signature squelchy bass, and two repeated and distorted samples: one is a rhythmic vocal line saying 'Bow E3', and the other is a synthesised string sound. The glitch-like repetition and cutting of both samples creates a relentless effect ('B-B-B-B-Bow E3'). The latter sounds like an inescapable wall of sound, with short reverbera-tions implying impact, as if the listener is repeatedly banging into a wall, unable to overcome the repetition. The bass's distortion—which intensifies in the middle section between 01:35 and 01:45—can be heard as a sonic representation of reaching the limit of available space. At times the bass rhythm speeds up in time with the relentlessly reset 'Bow E- Bow E- Bow E-' sample. There are no echoes or long, sustained notes in the music, and nothing to suggest open space. (Remember, grime production has always involved using and manipulating digital software and samples rather than recording live instruments in the 'real' space of a studio. Similarly, grime artists have always made music designed to sound good through personal headphones, in people's bedrooms, and in busy nightclubs, not in grand concert halls, festival venues or stadiums.) Instead, there are lots of short, sharp bursts of sound bouncing into and past each other. The track is an example of grime's unruly use of compression and distortion, foregoing a 'balanced'-sounding mix in favour of a more hectic and intense combina-tion of sounds that seem to hint at music's material limits. It is the kind of musical texture that Dale Chapman describes as somehow simultaneously full and flat: 'a flat plane of unrelenting sound that denies depth, perspec-tive, relief' (Chapman, 2008, 165). The different digitally produced, artifi-cial-sounding aspects of the instrumental are heard as somehow unrelated; rather than a harmonious or natural totality of sound there is a sense of different sonic features at different frequencies being forced to share the same condensed space, which creates a hectic effect.

Wiley's rapping style accentuates this claustrophobic intensity. 'Bow E3' is, like many grime tracks, relatively fast at 140 beats per minute (bpm), and although rappers from other genres might choose to hold longer notes and/or leave more space between lines over such a fast beat, here Wiley fills all available space with clipped, fast-paced vocals. This includes syllables that do not flow together, especially the repeated staccato delivery of 'Bow-E-three', with each syllable clearly distinguished. (Grime artists often forego smooth flow: AJ Tracey commonly emphasises the change from one syllable to another by using 'a' rather than 'an' for words that begin with a vowel sound. Jme similarly favours the staccato sounds of 'did a E' and 'ya eyeball', rather than the more flowing 'did an E' and 'your eyeball', on his 2011 track '96 Fuckries'. Jme also fills all the space in that track by rapping continuously for the full 02:25, with no introduction, chorus or outro.) Wiley uses the four syllables of 'anybody' when the three syllables of 'anyone' would have been a more natural choice in the line. During the first verse, between 0:28 and 0:55 there are 151 syllables (an average of 5.4 syllables per second), and in the most intense section between 0:34 and 0:47 he reaches almost six syllables per second. To put his pace in context: in US rap the average speed is 4.5 syllables per second, with the musical accompaniments averaging between 80 and 110 bpm (Condit-Schultz, 2016, 133–5). The contrast is even starker in relation to the verses of three other popular songs from different genres released in the same year. The R&B song 'Bleeding Love' by Leona Lewis has just under two syllables per second. Take That's epic pop hit 'Rule the World' is just under one syllable per second. 'Chasing Cars' by the indie band Snow Patrol includes just over 0.6 syllables per second in the verse. Wiley raps ten syllables in the time it takes Snow Patrol to sing one. He draws attention to the limits of the available space by filling it completely.

The sense of spatial limitation is intensified by Wiley's flow and verse structure. Almost every line ends with a repetition of 'E3':

Listen, my name's Wiley, I come from
Oh-seven-nine-six-one-eight-nine-seven-oh-three-three, I'm so E3
The whole of E3's got so much talent, I hope you see
I know E3 so well, if you ask me Wiley speaks for the whole of E3
You can't say that, Scorcher won't make anybody bow to his foot, I ain't
Wolf Pack
Boy Better Know E3, won't accept another doughnut MC disrespect E3
I'm always tryna rep ends but certain friends on ends they don't know E3

'Cos when it's reppin' time I show E3
We made the genre everybody's on but it's all come from Bow E3
It's Wiley AKA Eski-Boy I'm from Bow E3

The effect of repeatedly returning to 'E3' despite rapping so many words, to keep coming back to the same point, is to produce a pronounced lack of momentum. Or, rather, the internal variation within rhythmic repetition becomes the motivating, driving force of the track, and Wiley's rapped 'Bow E3's syncopate in interesting combinations with the 'Bow E3's of the glitch sample. The track does not build to a climax; rather, the same point is made again and again with varying intensity. In the first verse quoted above, Wiley begins by saying he is from E3, and he ends by saying he is from E3. This emphasis on intensity through repetition is characteristic of the grime genre more generally. This may be a function of what Anders Reuter refers to as the 'loop-paradigm' of the FruityLoops music production software often used by grime artists, in which the creative musical process is 'less about inscriptional value of musical material' than 'an ongoing adjustment, [or] manipulation' of material (Reuter, 2022a, 118). This entails, for the grime producer, a focus on timbral variation and complexity—'shaping sounds' (Reuter, 2022b, 60)—rather than melodic development. It entails manipulation of the micro-details of different sonic elements that must work in relation. Early grime MCs such as Wiley also grew their audiences through performing live at raves, where their aim was often to generate a highpoint of intensity (ideally enough to achieve a 'reload' from the DJ) rather than some kind of linear development. Grime is one of several influential twenty-first-century genres that is 'modular rather than teleological' in style, and 'treats rhythm and timbre (and not pitch, as is traditionally the case) as the primary organizational and expressive elements of a song' (R. James, 2015, 1; 11). We should understand Wiley's repetition of 'E3'—his using of that postcode reference as the structure and rhythmic driver of the track—as part of his method of expressing his 'level of resolution' or intense commitment to the local.

Despite Wiley's recent disgrace, his contributions to the early development of grime are widely acknowledged. He pioneered many of the genre's characteristic features. 'Bow E3' represents the genre well, as do his other, more collaborative yet still E3-focused tracks such as 'E3 Talent' (feat. Maverick) and 'E3 Link Up' (feat. All in One, Black Rain and Mega). Both these use a flattened, reverb-less, distinctly 'digital' or platform-game-style sound in the bass and drums that also creates a sense of spatial enclosure. But there are plenty of other grime artists who produce a similar effect with similar musical features. Stormzy's 2019 track 'Wiley Flow', for example, emphasises many of the elements of Wiley's style that became definitive of the grime genre. More Fire Crew's 'Oi' (2001)—which has been called the first grime song (Charles, 2016)—is built out of the same tinny high-hat rhythm and 'glitchy' sample repetition. The attack, pace and staccato style of rapping can be heard on Ghetts' 'Artillery', in which he rarely stops to take a breath, and most famously on the intensely clipped verses of Dizzee Rascal's 'Jus' a Rascal'. Dizzee ends each line of the first verse abruptly in time with the beat, with absolutely no sustained notes or echo, which exemplifies grime's tendency to create a sense of filling sonic space right up to its strict limits. In the third and final verse ('I'm streetwise with the phat guys, so spectize, make the whole crew capsize, slap guys …'), Dizzee reaches a crescendo of frustrated intensity, with the frequency of rhymes increasing, just as Wiley created a similar effect by increasing the number of mentions of 'E3' in a line. This is grime's famously 'relentless' vocal style (Charles, 2019, 107). Wiley's repetition of line-endings is also common in the genre more generally, such as in Roll Deep's 'When I'm 'Ere'. Every verse line of that track ends 'when I'm 'ere', with the same sense of relentless intensity created, especially in Manga's rapidly staccato verse ('critical with every syllable when I'm 'ere') and when Roachee increases the repetition frequency in the final verse:

> When I boom when I'm 'ere, when I jag when I'm 'ere
> Duck when I'm 'ere, tuck-tuck when I'm 'ere
> When I'm 'ere bring heat, I'm a G when I'm 'ere

This feature of grime—to intensify a track with increased rhyme frequency and repetition, rather than to use structural or melodic development such as key changes to 'break through' or reach a higher level or sense of closure/conclusion—exemplifies the genre's commitment to the postcode scale, its intensely local level of resolution.

But to fully understand the scalar significance of the genre's 'local'-ness, it is necessary to understand how grime is heard and used by its listeners and fans. Although I disagree with Woods (2020, 298) that grime 'remains largely unresearched', I agree with his suggestion that more research is needed into 'how the audiences that consume grime music engage with the spaces of grime' (Woods, 2020, 309). This kind of attention to how grime is heard is necessary for fully appreciating 'the new forms of power associated with grime' including 'the influences of grime on society and space, and how it may influence the ways in which its fans navigate the city, the spaces they occupy, and their overarching sense of place' (ibid.). Here I pursue this line of research by examining how a particular track in the grime tradition has been used as a place-specific protest song, focusing on the political purposes it has been put to. By focusing on moments when ostensibly apolitical songs become explicitly and directly involved in political campaigns—when political organisations adopt them as their anthems, or when street demonstrators sing and perform them in pursuit of political outcomes—it is possible to appreciate the power of grime's postcode scale.

The use of grime music in political protest has been widely noted and in some cases lamented (see Thompson & Biddle, 2013), but it pays to focus on a specific example: the role of Nadia Rose's 2016 track 'Skwod' in antifascist protest in Croydon on the southern edge of London. Rose was born in 1993 in Croydon. Her viral music videos have all been set in and around Croydon, and while her style has more in common with commercial R&B, Jamaican Dancehall and US hip-hop than earlier generations of grime artists, Rose's music nevertheless stands in the grime tradition of representing the neighbourhoods she grew up in, featuring heavy use of London slang and humour in her rapping, plus electronic samples and familiar squelchy bass. Lyrically, she develops grime's tendency to directly address perceived critics and to elevate apparently petty squabbles to the level of a poetic battle. For example, her 2016 breakthrough 'Station' is a sparsely produced track based around a skittish, stop-start beat and a dextrous, fast-paced rap exploring travel-related disputes.

'Station' is an example of how Rose's music explores the nature of places that are characterised by their relationships with and (dis)connections to the nearby metropolis. In the video, Rose raps on the rail tracks and platform at Chipstead, a suburban commuter station in the 'Stockbroker Belt', six train stops south from Croydon. Croydon itself is sometimes called an 'edge city', as it functions as a kind of border between inner city and rural, between urban and extra-urban; a 'post-suburban gateway' with a highly contested identity (Phelps et al., 2006, 185). It is a key junction on the route carrying commuters from central London to England's leafy Home Counties, although it is an administrative Borough of London and a large and populous town in its own right, with its own non-London postcode (CR0) and a town centre surrounded by 'sub-suburbs'. Croydon is a contested space representing the 'edge' of London in a more figurative and political sense too. It is not a conventional suburb or marginalised neighbourhood—it has not much in common with The Beatles' suburban pastoral, nor with the 'Status Symbol Land' skewered by the Monkees, nor with the mundane landscapes of middle-class malaise mocked by Radiohead and Everything But The Girl, and nor is it the ghettoised neighbourhood of resistance valorised by N.W.A.—but it has nevertheless been implicated in national debates about what a suburb should be. Croydon is home to the British Home Office's Visas and Immigration headquarters, where migrants seeking the legal right to live in the UK are obliged to attend and at which they are sometimes detained by Border Force officers. It is the kind of highly politicised 'immigrant gateway community' that has become a key site of pro- and anti-immigrant activism (Carpio et al., 2011, 189). It is therefore a local site of national significance, functioning both as an administrative border and as a symbol of the British state's immigration policy. Croydon has also been the scene of high-profile racist attacks (see Gilroy, 2012; Back, 2015). For right-wing nationalist politicians and campaign groups, Croydon is a key battleground, a site for defining the parameters of London and even the borders of the nation. It is in this context that fans have heard the political potential of the postcode-scale of Rose's grime.

Rose's biggest track is 'Skwod' (2016), which was accompanied by a viral YouTube video produced by Reece Proctor. But its political potential was not immediately and universally realised. Rose performs a version of it, albeit with the swearwords and drug references censored, in a commercial video for a multinational cosmetics brand featuring choreographed dancers in front of a generic central London cityscape. The 'Skwod' video itself looks almost like an advertisement for Adidas clothing, as Rose and her backing dancers are wearing coordinated Adidas tracksuits and shoes. Rose has also been the face and voice of a marketing campaign for a credit card in a commercial video that features her own generically uplifting track 'Make it Happen'. Moreover, 'Skwod' has a broadly feminist message celebrating a group or 'skwod' of women, but with its lyrical focus on small-scale criminality and partying it is not obviously or explicitly radically political in content. Even if they lack an explicitly political message, some songs have radical semantic import through a kind of 'diagnostic' power to highlight the causes of problems (see Murphy, 2019), but Rose's lyrics seem to lack even this. Nor does 'Skwod' have the angry, riotous, punk or otherwise strongly emotional energy of other grime tracks that have been used in political protest (Fisher, 2012; see also Brown, 2016; Halberstam, 2019). It does not particularly sound like the frustrated expression of the oppressed. Many of its stylistic features are common in commercial, radio-friendly pop music and as such it probably fits into the category of the 'sonically normative' (Halberstam, 2019, 248). Rose's music seems to be 'entirely complicit with its status as a market commodity' (Thompson & Biddle, 2013, 4) and any political content is expressed through the unassuming 'currency of pop' (Anohni quoted in Murphy, 2019, 219)—although of course many of the most effective protest songs have historically followed the conventions of popular or folk genres that have emerged organically from working-class communities (Martinez, 1997; Roscigno et al., 2002; Bierman, 2013; Turner, 2013). Simply put, Rose does not present herself according to the Woody Guthrie or Billy Bragg model of the protest singer, and 'Skwod' is not obviously a protest song. The song has, however, been put to radical political ends by the intersectional feminist activist group Sisters Uncut, who use it as the soundtrack to campaign videos and have commonly played and sung along to it at their political events and protests.

Sisters Uncut is an influential direct action group that has been widely discussed by scholars interested in innovative and intersectional approaches to feminist political organising (see Evans, 2016; Freedman, 2018; Ishkanian & Peña Saavedra, 2019). Sara Ahmed, for example, notes the value of their intersectional approach to issues of domestic violence that crucially takes account of 'racism, including state racism, immigration, detention, poverty, unemployment, the erosion of the welfare state, all those structures that distribute vulnerability and fragility unevenly to populations' (Ahmed, 2017, 211). Sisters Uncut organise around a 'shared otherness' and, as Lucy Freedman (2018, 238) explains, 'Their activism serves as a thread to hold together the oppressions and demands of a huge range of people, united in their experience of oppression as women.' The chant of 'sisters united will never be defeated' is commonly heard at their events. Their direct action approach often involves highly visible or disruptive interventions in public space, and this often involves the use of music and song. In November 2021, Sisters Uncut occupied London's Royal Courts of Justice to protest police violence against women. They chanted 'Freedom! Freedom! All these racist, sexist cops, we don't need 'em, need 'em!' When, in September 2016, the group occupied Hackney

Town Hall in East London to protest against the local council's housing policy, Sisters Uncut sang along to a modified version of Rihanna's 'Bitch Better Have My Money'. The chorus became 'You better keep your promise! Fill those empty council homes!' They also blocked London's Waterloo Bridge in November 2016 to protest cuts to domestic violence services, and then it was Rose's 'Skwod' that was heard prominently, and with its original lyrics.[2]

'Skwod' has long been the unofficial anthem of the South East London branch of Sisters Uncut and it has soundtracked several of their campaign videos. Rose herself endorsed the group's use of her song when Sisters Uncut used it to, in their words, 'fight the fash' in Croydon.[3] This was in the context of the May 2017 protest in Croydon organised by the far-right anti-immigration organisation the South East Alliance, who were campaigning outside an administrative office of the British Home Office that symbolised the British state's immigration policies. This was an example of a wider trend of reactionary, nativist activism projects that see themselves 'at the frontlines of a rescaled national boundary' and are focused on rescaling political power and claiming authority over immigration policy and practice at a local (rather than national or supranational) level (Varsanyi, 2011, 295). Sisters Uncut joined other antifascist groups endorsing a 'no borders' immigration policy to organise a counter-protest that was well attended and widely publicised under the hashtag #DefendCroydon. The effect of this contentious protest in Croydon was of a high-profile battle over 'who has the right to determine who can and cannot live in the suburb and under what conditions' (Carpio et al., 2011, 189). It was, in essence, a battle to be heard, to be seen and to disrupt in this symbolic

[2] In one video posted on the @SistersUncut Twitter account (20 November 2016), a group of women are seen dancing and singing along to the first verse and chorus of the song. In another video posted by the International Business Times (@IBTimesUK, 20 November 2016), 'Skwod' is heard in the background while a representative of Sisters Uncut is being interviewed.

[3] A video showing Sisters Uncut members dancing exuberantly to 'Skwod' was posted by @selsistersuncut on 6 May 2017 along with the text: 'The unofficial Sisters Anthem being used to fight the fash #DefendCroydon @nadiarosemusic'. Nadia Rose (@nadiarosemusic) quote-tweeted this approvingly: 'haha sick! I was just in Croydon getting arrested (unrelated) [laughing-crying emoji] and someone walked past n said my song was playing @ the protest [three red heart emojis] #SKWOD'. On the same day she tweeted the same '#DefendCroydon' hashtag. Others endorsed Sisters' Uncut's use of the song, such as @TheTungMagazine, who quote-tweeted the original @selsistersuncut post by adding, 'Yes yes! There's no better use for "Skwod" than this #DefendCroydon'.

suburban or edge city location of national significance, and a contest over different models or practices of inclusion and exclusion. Fellow South London grime artist Stormzy's track 'Big For Your Boots' (2017)—which generates a characteristically grime intensity against those who 'wanna come round here like a badboy'—was also heard at the same protest. It obviously has what Jeffrey Boakye (2018) describes as grime's agitprop-esque confrontational sound. But 'Skwod', which lacks that, featured most prominently and generated the strongest reaction from the protestors.

Why 'Skwod'? Most straightforwardly, Sisters Uncut may have heard the intersectional-feminist political potential in some of the song's key lyrics:

> I'm rollin' ten girl up in that skwod
> Fuckin' with my skwod? I think not
> Me and my bitches we roll deep
> And we always got green
> So we pretty much peas in a pod
> [...]
> Some girl are braided, some girl are in cornrows
> But still gon' dread if we have to
> The heart is built like a statue
> [...]
> Cause if my bitches need me there, well I'm comin'
> And if I ain't gotta wish it, I'm runnin'
> I do it for 'em, it ain't nothin', skwoddy

In these passages Rose plays on the 'roll deep' phrase, already adopted by the Roll Deep grime crew discussed above, to describe a squad or crew of women who look out for each other and are not to be fucked with. She references the different hairstyles of black women—braids, cornrows, dreadlocks—in a way that may chime with the intersectional and anti-racist concerns of Sisters Uncut. She also mentions South London locations and her accent and slang provide an appropriate place specificity. The track's production, too—especially the way the introductory and closing synth lines pan percussively between left and right in stereo as if bouncing between tall buildings—evokes a sense of space that reinforces the urban scenes depicted in the music video. (This panned synth line also features under the 'that what? That skwod' refrain, creating a subtle sense of spatial enclosure around the chorus.) And in the video for 'Skwod', Rose leads a group of women as they dance down a densely built Croydon high street.

The video—which has had over 13 million views on YouTube—is a promi-nent example of the tradition of grime videos showing the artists appropri-ating or taking up space in the city (Woods, 2020), especially in sites of significance to a particular postcode-locality, often alongside diverse groups, crews or 'skwods' representing oppressed gender identities and/or races. Sisters Uncut's repurposing of 'Skwod' as an intersectional femi-nist anthem about the collective reclaiming of urban space and public rights for marginalised groups could be seen as a musical practice of reclaiming the 'right to the city' (following Lefebvre, 1996; Mitchell, 2003; Carpio et al., 2011; Johnson, 2013). It certainly supported their praxis of taking up or intervening in a politicised public sphere, and of reasserting the political agency of racialised, migrantised or otherwise oppressed people over (sub)urban space.

Even it does not deliver direct political messages, like Guthrie's 'This Land is Your Land' and Bragg's 'Power in a Union', 'Skwod' nevertheless has some of the traditional elements of a protest song. Lyrically it has sev-eral chant-friendly call-and-response or question-and-answer elements ('That what? That skwod'; 'Fuckin' with my Skwod? I think not') that might be considered as part of a 'local repertoire' of musical repetition used in political struggle (Gilbert, 2007, 426). There is a similar call-and-response effect to the coupled phrases in the bass and synth verse accom-paniment, and rhythmically it is suited to marching or dancing (see Manabe, 2019). All of these make it amenable to use in contemporary public protests. Its musical features give it feminist import too. The pro-duction allows Rose to take on a heroic, powerful persona while nonethe-less presenting herself as the embodiment, or rather the uniting figure, of a community of women. There is minimal content in the upper end of the production that might mask the vocal line. This is a sparer production than most grime. It has a staccato synth line and of course grime's squelchy bass, but it resembles the relatively minimal and space-filled, start-stop production of hip-hop pioneers Timbaland and Missy Elliot (see Chapman, 2008). This means she can rap in a relaxed manner and adopt the unbothered-by-authority attitude she communicates in the lyrics (which is especially suited to the context of a counter-protest against angry, shout-ing men). With the exception of a few sections of increased intensity (such as when the verse builds towards the chorus), she is not obliged to battle with or stand out over other high-frequency sounds. The laid-back per-sona that Rose adopts is partly a result of the fact that she *does not* fill all the available sonic space. Moreover, the few moments when her syllables-per-second ratio increases ('I do it for them, it ain't nothin', Skwoddy!') seem to signal the intensity of her commitment to the skwod. Rose is, as she puts it, 'with my team'. Sisters Uncut heard this political, feminist potential in the track.

One might interpret this as a case of what José Esteban Muñoz (1999) calls 'disidentification' (whereby minoritised groups appropriate aspects of mainstream culture for specific cultural-political ends), or of 'queer use' in Ahmed's (2019) terms. Queer use in a basic sense refers to 'how things can be used in ways other than for which they were intended or by those other than for whom they were intended' (Ahmed, 2019, 199). Moreover, it entails 'releasing a potentiality that already resides in things given how they have taken shape. Queer use could be what we are doing when we release that potential' (ibid., 200). Specifically, queer use is 'to linger on the material qualities of that which you are supposed to pass over; it is to *recover* a potential from materials that have been left behind' (ibid., 207–8; italics in original). Ahmed's emphasis on the *potential* that is activated by users who linger on the specific qualities of something that is otherwise overlooked fits well with the relationship between 'Skwod' and Sisters Uncut. Indeed, Ahmed (2019) uses Sisters Uncut's policies of disruptive public protest and squatting or occupying as examples of queer use via *the disruption of usage*. So, contrary to the interpretations of advertising executives and others who might hear apolitical mainstream popular music and use it for their purposes, Sisters Uncut seemed to find that Nadia Rose's music was perfectly suited to contemporary political projects relating to the defence and valorisation of politically contested (sub)urban space from an intersectional feminist perspective. They lingered on its material qualities and heard its high-resolution detail, thereby realising its potential.

In addition to the aforementioned aspects of 'Skwod' that function well as a protest song, there is a scale-related element of its specific appeal to Sisters Uncut that requires further elaboration. Specifically, 'Skwod' features various musical techniques of *inclusion and exclusion* that mean the song suits both the intersectional premise of South East London Sisters Uncut and the specific context of the #DefendCroydon antifascist protest. Firstly, 'Skwod' does have an obviously communal, inclusive element. It demonstrates what Bill Rolston (2001, 51) calls 'pop's ability to speak for and to a community', especially a community based around resistance to a dominating or reactionary power. There are the aforementioned lyrical details that celebrate the collective, plus the call-and-response features that invite audience participation. There are also the backing dancers in the video: more and more join as the performance goes on. Moreover, for a track by a solo artist, it is notable that 'Skwod' has the feel and sound of a collective, community-building anthem (see Gupta-Carlson, 2010). This is achieved in part through the subtle layering of vocals in the chorus and even the glitch-like doubling or rhythmic repetition of certain words in the verse, especially at the endings and beginnings of lines (e.g. 'she's shit and she's wack (wack) / (they-they) they talk all that chat …'). This creates the collective effect that backing singers or hype women or men might otherwise provide. It is important to note, though, that the song is not inclusive to all, and the context of its performance cannot be construed in the simple terms of resistance versus dominance. The #DefendCroydon protest was a clash between at least three opposing groups: the fascist protestors, the antifascist protestors, and the police. Sisters Uncut, who campaign against both anti-immigrant fascist movements *and* police and state violence, sat in a specific position in that context. As Judith Butler (2014) has pointed out, different bodies are policed in public space in different ways, such that different groups experience public demonstrations differently. Sisters Uncut see themselves as opposing diverse forms of state and non-state domination, so their choice of protest song needs to reflect that position.

Grime artists are experts at positioning themselves in relation to diverse external threats or groups. Lyrics addressing perceived disses or opponents are common in rap-based genres and especially prominent in grime. Many grime tracks establish the MC's identity against hostile interpretations of them: *some people say X about me—well, it's not true, and let me tell you why!* This is the premise of Stormzy's breakthrough hit 'Shut Up', and of course Wiley's 'Bow E3' begins with an expression of incredulity that 'certain man tryna say like I don't rep for E3 … it's amazing that you can say that!' It is notable that 'the cops' feature as antagonists in Rose's 'Skwod', as well as other unidentified enemies who apparently talk shit about her. She uses this technique to address and produce a specific audience, and to incite or even perform an audience response or mobilise a specific public (see Gupta-Carlson, 2010). Take, for example, the track's opening lines:

Guess who's back? 'But you never left!'
Yes I did, I rose from the dead
And now I'm here to kill them with flows
And some punchlines that'll go over your head
Huh, turn back, I'm a caution ahead

> I'm your worst nightmare stood over your bed
> So dem girl trya call me
> But I smell defeat like a hole in your creps
> Wow, she's sick and she's bad
> She sings and she raps
> She's shit and she's wack
> They talk all that chat
> But when they see me don't speak none of that

She begins by questioning the listener directly ('guess who's back?') and ventriloquising their answer ('but you never left!') in a higher-pitched voice. Rose seems to be hostile to 'you' and to 'them' or what 'they' say, while identifying strongly with 'dem' (i.e. the skwod). Indeed, grime artists such as Wiley, Stormzy and Nadia Rose tend to address and produce a specific, by-no-means-all-inclusive audience: the music is open only to those who identify with it, and it excludes those who do not. This surely resonates with Sisters Uncut's intersectional inclusivity, as Ishkanian and Peña Saavedra (2019) describe it. The group's 'boundary making'—their exclusion of those who identify as men—is crucial in their efforts 'to bring to the fore previously marginalised voices' (ibid., 993) and even to campaign for a 'no borders' geopolitical settlement. Likewise, the police and fascist protestors should not 'get' or feel included in their musical performance. As Turner (2013) and Roscigno et al. (2002) have shown, this *selectiveness* in terms of who gets to 'get' the song and who gets included in the 'we' or 'us' has long been important for performers of protest songs.

Another technique of inclusion and exclusion that Rose uses to great effect is humour. The opening lines contain several jokes. 'Rose from the dead' is a straightforward pun referencing her own first name, but other comic lines will not be understood by all. 'I smell defeat like a hole in your creps' relies on the audience knowing that 'creps' is slang for 'shoes'. Some of the jokes will 'go over your head', and only those familiar with drug slang ('green', 'blunts', 'Mary Jane', 'Molly', 'zoot') will appreciate all of the song's comic qualities. Just as (sometimes abusive) humour and irreverence often function in protest songs that need to both 'caustically accuse the oppressors [and] enthusiastically uplift the oppressed' (Shonekan, 2009, 136), so Rose's music fits into this tradition of songs that are both 'inwardly uplifting and outwardly accusatory' through ridicule, sarcasm and a collective voice constructed around feminist jokes-and-punchlines (ibid., 137; see also Woldu, 2019). 'Skwod' plays with jokes addressed at key targets; jokes that only some are intended to get. This selective inclusion and exclusion is also heard in the structure of the song. The verses, which in lyrical terms are for the most part addressed to a hostile other, seem to intensify through louder vocals, more dense instrumentation, and especially the compression and filter sweeps common in hip-hop and electronic dance music. At the end of the verse, these timbral features build energy and momentum, but instead of a soaring chorus at a higher pitch (as in most conventional pop songs), there is a 'drop' or breakdown. In the drop, a common feature of contemporary EDM-inspired music production, a rapid 'deintensification of register feels and functions as an *intensification* of sonic energy', akin to the power of sudden deceleration rather than acceleration (R. James, 2015, 36). So as the track shifts down to bass frequencies and the stereo synth line surrounds the repeated refrain of 'that what? That skwod', there is a chorus whose power comes through a drop in intensity. This may be disorientating or alienating for many casual listeners, but it signals, for those included, the turn inwards to celebrate and strengthen the collective. This relates to the kind of dancing and chanting seen in the tweeted video of 'Skwod' playing at the protest. If we follow Pat Noxolo (2018, 807) in paying greater attention to the dance, 'choreography' and 'diverse movement repertoires' of 'cultural signification' in urban street protests, we see in this case that not everyone in shot or even in the antifascist protest group is actually dancing. Plenty remain still or looking at their phones. Of course, the police officers stand unmoved and watchful. This is not some kind of material-affective sonic force that moves bodies spontaneously and equally. Rather, there is one group dancing together, and their bodies are turned inwards, towards each other, while they gesture aggressively outward, towards the diverse groups to which they are opposed. This dancing group sings the chorus communally, together, with each other, but also past the line of police towards the far-right demonstrators. Their musical performance signals both solidarity among a collective *and* hostility to diverse external enemies, just as 'Skwod' incorporates a complex mix of inclusive and exclusive elements, and just as the grime genre has always played musically and politically with the borders and limits of inclusion and belonging.

So, to sum up: if grime is a 'local' genre, it is a local defined by permeable boundaries and an uneven, modernist, postcode scale. Grime artists are concerned with intense renderings of the local, but this local is not purely defensive or nostalgic. It resembles, in this respect, the 'global sense of place' or 'global sense of the local' that Doreen Massey (1993a, b) describes: it goes beyond any local-global counterposition and instead defines 'local' places by the nature of their external relations—to whom or what they are (dis)connected. Grime, in this interpretation, is involved in producing a different kind of 'local'. In a context in which people's legitimacy of belonging is questioned at multiple scales, grime intervenes in a battle between different kinds of belonging and different ideals of the local, the urban and the national. And while Sisters Uncut have used grime and heard its potential in this specific context of a South London political protest, they have done so in a way that targets the global system of state bordering and therefore has global implications for the scalar category of 'the national'. In this sense, the use of 'Skwod' discussed here is an example of how the solidaristic use of music may contribute to the production of 'unbordered homelands' (Bhowmik & Rogaly, 2023). Indeed, Croydon is not simply a suburban or local case: it functions symbolically and practically as a national boundary and as the contested border of the 'inner city' and its associated connotations for anti-immigrant campaigners. In Croydon, grime has taken part in the battle over 'who has the right to determine who can and cannot live in the suburb'—or in a place defined at any scale—'and under what conditions' (Carpio et al., 2011, 189). It comes from 'the spatial margins' (Woods, 2020, 304) and it acts at the boundary where (the nature of) place is made.

Grime has this spatial-political function because of its postcode scale. This scale is not necessarily, as Bramwell (2015, 125) has it, more 'restricted' than others, but it is *selective* in a different way, emphasising different features, and it does concern complex procedures of inclusion and exclusion. As this chapter has shown, Rose uses several musical techniques to exclude hostile external groups and simultaneously to address an explicitly included audience. She demonstrates how grime functions as something that is open to some and potentially not to others—or at least not in the same way. While some listeners are not intended to 'get' it, her music is open for certain kinds of use and interpretation by audiences who linger over its material details. It was not meant to be universally accessible nor to express generally applicable truths, which is perhaps why it does not seem 'global'. It is selectively available as a political resource. It shows a sensitivity to what Ahmed (2017, 211) describes as 'all those structures that distribute vulnerability and fragility unevenly to populations'. It is a creative engagement with what White (2020, 250) calls the 'bounded territories that are border patrolled by private security' and the 'heavily guarded structures of wealth and privilege'. 'Skwod' enables alliance-building between those with a shared experience of such structures. Grime artists produce music that is distinctly 'local' yet heard as meaningful to the marginalised: 'to kids all across the country living in similar circumstances' (DJ Target, 2018, 114), and to people in 'the urban margins across the world' or 'ghetto wherever' (Hancox, 2018, 162). Global listeners relate to and unite around grime's level of resolution: the squelchy bass, the timbral complexity and intensification within a loop logic, and the other techniques used to signify grime's commitment to and identification with the local community.

This selectivity is part of grime's postcode scale. It is common to assume that adopting a 'local' scale simply means focusing on an area of a specific size, but more often it is about drawing attention to certain features rather than others, or making some things perceivable and others not. This is already the case with, say, the national scale, in which not everything of or within a nation is included. Likewise, there are processes that occur pretty much evenly across the world that would not be understood as 'global' or included in a global overview. So grime also works with a scalar system in which not everywhere or everyone is included. This functions, implicitly, as a critique of the selectivity of the existing systems. It also functions politically because of its level of resolution—it has a granular detail appropriate for the densely populated areas of London, with the postcode symbolising a scale that does not apply evenly over space but instead organises spatial units according to their characteristics. And this selectivity means that experience and understanding of the music varies. The Sisters Uncut protestors were able to hear and express 'Skwod's political potential in the context of defending their suburb against far-right organisations and a broader right-wing political discourse. They were positioned to linger over the track's high-resolution details and had a richer, more specialised understanding of the song than, say, the marketing executives who used it to sell cosmetics. This intensely local listening, too, is a part of grime's postcode scale, and it supports Lila Ellen Gray's (2016) observation that it takes sensitivity to local particularity and to small aesthetic details for a song to move to a political context and catalyse protest. To understand grime's politics and what Woods (2020, 309) calls 'the new forms of power associated with grime', it is necessary to look beyond the semantic content of the artists' statements and lyrics, and to consider in addition the aesthetic details that are heard as political by specific audiences. Crucially, grime artists are not only 'organic intellectuals' in Gramscian terms (see Charles, 2018), but also musical 'specialists of space', following Lefebvre (1991). Their music is not just defined in relation to space, or referring to specific places, or even sounding like certain kinds of locations; instead, their music intervenes in space and works to produce a new kind of place. Theirs is a cultural practice that involves the construction of new geographies and new spatial relationships at and through the postcode scale. It is crucial to understand this if we are to meet Woods' (2020, 309) challenge of fully appreciating 'the influences of grime on society and space'.

The features pioneered by the earlier generation of grime artists, such as Dizzee Rascal, Roll Deep and Wiley, have come to signify the intensity of the postcode scale in a way that Rose and grime fans could use. As this chapter has shown, part of the reason the genre is interpreted as intensely/ microscopically/hyper local is that grime tracks make an aesthetic feature of boundaries, by returning to the same point constantly and with increasing intensity, or by emphasising how boundaries are permeable and differentially policed. It is not just the MCs' rapping speed, with their high syllables-per-second rate relative to other genres, but their frequently clipped, staccato style, with no long sustained notes or space between lines, that creates the hectic, relentless, breathless intensity that defines grime's 'level of resolution'. In addition, the glitch-like repetition and cutting of samples, as well as the repetition of rhymes, phrases and line-endings, often accentuates this effect of banging repeatedly against a barrier, of being bound and inescapably restricted, contributing to the sense that grime's local scale is distinctively intense in comparison with that of, say, The Beatles. Grime's is a non-nostalgic localism. Grime artists do not create a traditional, calm, bucolic or 'small' sense of the local, where something that is 'local' is somehow insignificant. Rather, Wiley performs the E3 postcode as a place of hectic energy, and his commitment to it is intense.

All of this is part of grime artists' political commitment to overlooked and contested spaces—the grimy margins, gaps and edges of urban life that require greater granularity and a higher level of resolution for their rendering—and their cultural exploration of places that are not taken to be nationally significant or globally connected. Nor do grime artists adopt a more *restricted* scale than other musicians, but they tend to artistically explore demarcation, particularism and spatial restriction rather than generalisation and universalism. Grime offers an aggregated accumulation of postcode-scale truths that speak in an intensely local aesthetic register to 'urban Britain' and 'ghetto wherever', rather than an attempt to break through beyond local experience or grasp towards universal truths. It is this more mainstream musical jump, from local experience to general claim, that is the focus of the next chapter.

REFERENCES

Adams, R. (2019). 'Home sweet home, that's where I come from, where I got my knowledge of the road and the flow from': Grime music as an expression of identity in postcolonial London. *Popular Music and Society, 42*(4), 438–455.
Ahmed, S. (2017). *Living a feminist life.* Duke University Press.
Ahmed, S. (2019). *What's the use? On the uses of use.* Duke University Press.
Back, L. (2015). Why everyday life matters: Class, community and making life livable. *Sociology, 49*(5), 820–836.
Bhowmik, M., & Rogaly, B. (2023). In search of unbordered homelands: Exploring the role of music in building affective internationalist politics of solidarity. *The Sociological Review, 71*(2), 406–423.
Bierman, B. (2013). Solidarity forever: Music and the labor movement in the United States. In J. C. Friedman (Ed.), *The Routledge history of social protest in popular music* (pp. 31–43). Routledge.
Boakye, J. (2018). *Hold tight: Black masculinity, millennials and the meaning of grime.* Turnaround.
Bramwell, R. (2015). *UK hip-hop, grime and the city: The aesthetics and ethics of London's rap scenes.* Routledge.
Brown, A. J. (2016). Above and below the streets: A musical geography of anti-nuclear protest in Tokyo. *Emotion, Space and Society, 20*, 82–89.
Butler, J. (2014). Bodily vulnerability, coalitions, and street politics. In *Differences in common* (pp. 97–119). Brill.
Carpio, G., Irazábal, C., & Pulido, L. (2011). Right to the suburb? Rethinking Lefebvre and immigrant activism. *Journal of Urban Affairs, 33*(2), 185–208.
Chapman, D. (2008). 'That ill, tight sound': Telepresence and biopolitics in post-Timbaland rap production. *Journal of the Society for American Music, 2*(2), 155–175.
Charles, M. (2016). Grime central!: Subterranean ground-in grit engulfing manicured mainstream spaces. In K. Andrews (Ed.), *Blackness in Britain* (pp. 89–100). Routledge.
Charles, M. (2018). Grime labour. Soundings, 68(68), 40–52. https://doi.org/10.3898/13626621882845673.
Charles, M. (2019). Grime and spirit: On a hype! *Open Cultural Studies, 3*(1), 107–125.

Cohen, S. (2012). Urban musicscapes: Mapping music-making in Liverpool. In L. Roberts (Ed.), *Mapping cultures: Place, practice, performance* (pp. 123–143). Palgrave Macmillan.

Condit-Schultz, N. (2016). MCFlow: A digital corpus of rap transcriptions. *Empirical Musicology Review, 11*(2), 124–147.

Evans, E. (2016). Intersectionality as feminist praxis in the UK. *Women's Studies International Forum, 59,* 67–75.

Fisher, M. (2012). Autonomy in the UK. *The Wire, 335,* 38–39.

Forman, M., 2002. The 'Hood Comes First: Race, Space, and Place in Rap and Hip-hop. Wesleyan University Press.

Freedman, L. (2018). A 'beautiful half hour of being a mere woman': The feminist subject and temporary solidarity. *Historical Materialism, 26*(2), 221–241.

Gilbert, S. (2007). Singing against apartheid: ANC cultural groups and the international anti-apartheid struggle. *Journal of Southern African Studies, 33*(2), 421–441.

Gilroy, P. (2012). 'My Britain is fuck all': Zombie multiculturalism and the race politics of citizenship. *Identities, 19*(4), 380–397.

Gray, L. E. (2016). Registering protest: Voice, precarity, and return in crisis Portugal. *History and Anthropology, 27*(1), 60–73.

Gupta-Carlson, H. (2010). Planet B-girl: Community building and feminism in hip-hop. *New Political Science, 32*(4), 515–529.

Halberstam, J. (2019). *Power in the darkness* and 'angry Atthis': Anthems, genres and the queer voice. In S. Fast & C. Jennex (Eds.), *Popular music and the politics of hope: Queer and feminist interventions* (pp. 247–257). Routledge.

Hancox, D. (2013). *Stand up tall: Dizzee rascal and the birth of grime.* Kindle Editions.

Hancox, D. (2018). *Inner city pressure: The story of grime.* HarperCollins.

Ishkanian, A., & Peña Saavedra, A. (2019). The politics and practices of intersectional prefiguration in social movements: The case of sisters uncut. *The Sociological Review, 67*(5), 985–1001.

James, R. (2015). *Resilience & melancholy: Pop music, feminism, neoliberalism.* John Hunt Publishing.

James, M. (2020). *Sonic intimacy: Reggae sound systems, jungle pirate radio and grime YouTube music videos.* Bloomsbury.

Johnson, G. T. (2013). *Spaces of conflict, sounds of solidarity: Music, race, and spatial entitlement in Los Angeles.* University of California Press.

Lefebvre, H. (1991). *The production of space.* Blackwell.

Lefebvre, H. (1996). *Writings on cities.* Blackwell.

Manabe, N. (2019). We Gon' be alright? The ambiguities of Kendrick Lamar's protest anthem. *Music Theory Online, 25*(1).

Marston, S. A. (2000). The social construction of scale. *Progress in Human Geography, 24*(2), 219–242.

Martinez, T. A. (1997). Popular culture as oppositional culture: Rap as resistance. *Sociological Perspectives, 40*(2), 265–286.

Massey, D. (1993a). A global sense of place. In A. Gray & J. McGuigan (Eds.), *Studying culture* (pp. 232–240). Edward Arnold.

Massey, D. (1993b). Power-geometry and a progressive sense of place. In J. Bird et al. (Eds.), *Mapping the futures: Local cultures, global change* (pp. 59–69). Routledge.

McCarthy, A. (2006). From the ordinary to the concrete: Cultural studies and the politics of scale. In M. White & J. Schwoch (Eds.), *Questions of method in cultural studies* (pp. 21–53). Blackwell.

Mitchell, D. (2002). Controlling space, controlling scale: Migratory labour, free speech, and regional development in the American West. *Journal of Historical Geography, 28*(1), 63–84.

Mitchell, D. (2003). *The right to the city: Social justice and the fight for public space.* Guilford Press.

Muñoz, J. E. (1999). *Disidentifications: Queers of color and the performance of politics.* University of Minnesota Press.

Murphy, M. (2019). Electro-pop as Trojan Horse: Hearing the call to arms in Anohni's *HOPELESSNESS.* In S. Fast & C. Jennex (Eds.), *Popular music and the politics of hope: Queer and feminist interventions* (pp. 217–230). Routledge.

Noxolo, P. (2018). Flat out! Dancing the city at a time of austerity. *Environment and Planning D: Society and Space, 36*(5), 797–811.

Phelps, N. A., Parsons, N., Ballas, D., & Dowling, A. (2006). The croydonisation of South London? In N. A. Phelps et al. (Eds.), *Post-suburban Europe: Planning and politics at the margins of Europe's capital cities* (pp. 172–196). Palgrave Macmillan.

Reuter, A. (2022a). Who let the DAWs out? The digital in a new generation of the digital audio workstation. *Popular Music and Society, 45*(2), 113–128.

Reuter, A. (2022b). Pop materialising: Layers and topological space in digital pop music. *Organised Sound, 27*(1), 59–68.

Rolston, B. (2001). 'This is not a rebel song': The Irish conflict and popular music. *Race & Class, 42*(3), 49–67.

Roscigno, V. J., Danaher, W. F., & Summers-Effler, E. (2002). Music, culture and social movements: Song and southern textile worker mobilization, 1929–1934. *International Journal of Sociology and Social Policy, 22*(1/2/3), 141–174.

Rose, T. (1989). Orality and technology: Rap music and Afro-American cultural resistance. *Popular Music & Society, 13*(4), 35–44.

Rose, T. (1994). *Black noise: Rap music and black culture in contemporary America.* Wesleyan University Press.

Shonekan, S. (2009). Fela's foundation: Examining the revolutionary songs of Funmilayo Ransome-Kuti and the Abeokuta market women's movement in 1940s Western Nigeria. *Black Music Research Journal, 29*(1), 127–144.

Smith, N. (2010). *Uneven development: Nature, capital, and the production of space*. University of Georgia Press.

Target, D. J. (2018). *Grime kids: The inside story of the global grime takeover*. Hachette.

Thompson, M., & Biddle, I. D. (2013). Introduction: Somewhere between the signifying and the sublime. In M. Thompson & I. D. Biddle (Eds.), *Sound, music, affect: Theorizing sonic experience* (pp. 1–23). Bloomsbury.

Turner, K. L. (2013). Sonic opposition: Protesting racial violence before civil rights. In J. C. Friedman (Ed.), *The Routledge history of social protest in popular music* (pp. 44–56). Routledge.

Varsanyi, M. W. (2011). Neoliberalism and nativism: Local anti-immigrant policy activism and an emerging politics of scale. *International Journal of Urban and Regional Research, 35*(2), 295–311.

White, J. (2017). Controlling the flow: How urban music videos allow creative scope and permit social restriction. *Young, 25*(4), 407–425.

White, J. (2019). Growing up in 'the ends': Identity, place and belonging in an urban East London neighbourhood. In S. Habib & M. R. M. Ward (Eds.), *Identities, youth and belonging: International perspectives* (pp. 17–33). Routledge.

White, J. (2020). *Terraformed: Young black lives in the inner city*. Repeater.

Woldu, G. H. (2019). 'Don't I look like a Halle Berry poster?': Humor and irony in women's hip hop. In T. M. Kitts & N. Baxter-Moore (Eds.), *The Routledge companion to popular music and humor* (pp. 339–345). Routledge.

Woods, O. (2020). The digital subversion of urban space: Power, performance and grime. *Social & Cultural Geography, 21*(3), 293–313.

CHAPTER 4

Musical Scale-Jumping: 'What a Wonderful World' from Lysekil to Lviv

Abstract Louis Armstrong's 'What a Wonderful World' exemplifies popular music's tendency and ability to build from the particular into the general—or to connect the personal to the universal. The lyrics' logical leap from local observation to general claim is accompanied by several musical features that enable this leap to be landed. The musical transition to what Édouard Glissant calls 'Whole-World thinking' also functions in various cover versions of the song, including politically charged live performances at a Swedish climate protest in 2019, and outside Lviv train station (and widely shared on social media) during Russia's ongoing invasion of Ukraine. This Armstrong classic shows the potential of what might be called musical 'scale jumping', following Neil Smith, reorienting audiences to new scales of political contest. It also exemplifies how cultural practices have long been involved in fusing relations between the experiential and the general, or between particular places and what Glissant calls the 'Whole-World'.

Keywords Louis Armstrong • What a Wonderful World • Climate protest • Jens Lekman • Protest song • Sweden • Ukraine

Listen to:
Louis Armstrong, 'What a Wonderful World' (1967)
Pianist at Lviv train station, 'What a Wonderful World' (2022)

© The Author(s) 2023   61
P. Dodds, *Music and the Cultural Production of Scale*,
https://doi.org/10.1007/978-3-031-36283-5_4

In March 2020 I attended a climate protest in Lysekil, Sweden. Demonstrators from across Sweden came to this town of some 8000 inhabitants on the west coast, at the tip of a peninsula north of Gothenburg, to protest against the expansion of an oil refinery there. It was wet and bitterly cold, and the politics of the event were not straightforward. The protestors—most of whom had come on coaches from Gothenburg organised by the environmental activist networks Extinction Rebellion, Greenpeace and Fridays For Future—did not seem popular with many of the locals in Lysekil. Banners, car horns and other hostile statements from passers-by made it clear that oil refinery expansion—which would bring more jobs to this community—was well-supported by at least some of the people and trades union organisers in the town. The Swedish oil company Preem has been a major employer there since it took over the refinery in 2003. Behind the 150 or so assembled protestors on Lysekil's Rosvikstorg was a clearly visible message posted on a hoarding by an association of local businesses: 'We cannot solve all climate problems with imports—Let Preem continue to develop our fuel' ('Vi kan inte lösa alla klimatproblem med import – Låt Preem fortsätta utveckla våra drivmedel'). The centre-right Moderate Party had organised a counter-demonstration in a nearby park. The atmosphere was tense. As with many big demonstrations, the event involved a series of political speeches interspersed with live music performances. One speaker proclaimed: 'Six hundred jobs are nothing compared to life on Earth' ('Sexhundra arbetstillfällen är ingenting mot livet på jorden'). The compere encouraged the crowd to 'dansa oss varm' ('dance ourselves warm') as punk-rock bands and dub-reggae artists played short sets, often with explicitly political lyrics.

In this context I want to discuss the performance at this protest by the Gothenburg-based singer-songwriter Jens Lekman. Lekman is another artist who demonstrates musical 'scalecraft'. An interest in different scales of cultural experience is evident in his approach to live shows and touring, as he produces and explores different levels of fan-performer intimacy. During the pandemic he embraced the 'compressed intimacy' of one-to-one performances with individual fans over Zoom on his 'Zoom jukebox' sessions, for example (see Dodds, 2021). For a Guest Studio Session streamed from the Nordic Watercolour Museum in Västra Götaland in April 2021 he requested submissions of fans' stories which he turned into songs and performed directly back to them over Zoom. The premise of his 2015 Living Room Tour was also that his songs that circulate globally and that are toured in large venues internationally could be transposed into a suburban living room with an intimate audience of a couple of dozen fans. Some of his song lyrics play with scalar themes: 'The End of the World is Bigger Than Love' (2012), for example, is an attempt to put personal heartbreak into perspective, while 'How We Met, The Long Version' (2017) plays with the kind of romantic story one might have to tell if one decided to take the Big Bang as the starting point. I have written elsewhere about his complex musical renderings of specific suburban spaces (Dodds, 2019), and he has written explicitly political songs about his home city of Gothenburg (see, e.g., 2011's 'Waiting For Kirsten'). However, in Lysekil Lekman announced to the crowd that he mostly writes love songs and that 'I have no protest songs' ('jag har inga protest songs'). He explained that he would instead select from a popular musical repertoire or canon a 'classic' appropriate for this occasion. The last song of his set was a version of Louis Armstrong's 'What a Wonderful World'.

This was an interesting song choice for a climate protest. It functioned as a political protest song—one that apparently motivated and united the assembled demonstrators—by virtue of its ability to connect the particular or local to the general or global. 'What a Wonderful World' exemplifies Western pop music's propensity to reach general truths from specific experiences, or to connect the local or experiential to some version of the universal. Much art does this, as Glissant (2020) points out. Cultural practices deploy a poetics or aesthetics of relation that 'leads us to conceive of the elusive "worldness"' of particular and emplaced experience (ibid., 12). This 'aesthetic of Relation' is, for Glissant, 'the search, wandering and often anxious, of conjunctions of forms and structures that allow an idea of the world' (ibid., 11; 19). Glissant's 'Whole-World thinking' comes through 'the intertwined poetics that allow me to sense how my place joins up with others, how without moving it ventures elsewhere, and how it carries me along in this immobile movement' (ibid., 74). It entails what he calls 'the *trace*, as opposed to systematic thought, [which] acts as a wandering that guides us. We know that the trace is what puts us, all of us, wherever we come from, in Relation' (ibid., 9). Further, 'Trace thought confirms the concept as movement, and relates it: gives its narrative, places it in relation, sings its relativity' (ibid., 50). Music makes this connection, putting personal experience and *the world* in relation, through its aesthetic qualities, and I suggest that 'What a Wonderful World' is a useful example for exploring how music can support the semantic meaning of lyrics that express precisely this connection.

The lyrical premise of 'What a Wonderful World' is relatively simple, and it stands in a tradition of pop songs that do broadly similar things lyrically and structurally. The singer makes simple, particular observations of things that we might understand as beautiful—green trees, blooming red roses, 'friends shaking hands' and so on—and seems to find in these evidence that the world is wonderful. The semantic relevance of this song to the politics of the climate protest are also relatively clear. The assembled audience are reminded of the beauty of the world as a whole, the maintenance of which is their explicit purpose for attending this event in an icy town square where the spring colours had still not arrived. In a basic sense, the audience are reminded of the bigger picture of their efforts and impelled by the singer to focus less on the local politics of the day than the ultimate environmental imperative, which is global in scale. It was, in Lysekil, a musical-poetic version of the message that 600 jobs here are less important than life on earth, and also that what happens here is fundamentally connected to the wider world. It may also be relevant that this Louis Armstrong song falls into a broad category of popular songs that appear almost placeless and timeless—endlessly reproduced and reinterpreted, and known, perhaps even word by word, by almost everybody familiar with Western popular music, such that the assembled protestors could grasp that meaning in the song's performance without having to listen closely to the lyrics.

This could be interpreted, following Smith (1996), as an example of musical 'scale jumping'. Smith describes how 'scale-jumping as a political strategy' entails intervening in the political geographies of a given context by '*remaking the geographical scale* of daily social and political intercourse' (Smith, 1996, 73; 65—italics in original). Mitchell (2002, 71) has similarly explored 'how social movements are able to "jump scale"' when they 'transform their actions from ones that impinge on processes at one scale to ones that are effective at other scales'. A device or technique that enables scale-jumping is one that allows the reconfiguration, rearticulation and recasting of political struggles at a different scale, and the rescaling of political power. As mentioned in the introduction, Smith's examples of artworks with this function were chosen because of their demonstrable practicality—they 'literally' gave people power over a new scale of social life (Smith, 1996, 66). Lekman's choice of protest song did not do that. It was, nevertheless, involved in the complex reconfiguration of that political protest that day. This is not simply because it gestured poetically towards the importance of a global perspective or because it could be practically used for this purpose. Rather, the ability of the song to recast the day's attention to a larger scale, and to assert the imbrication of the local with the wider world, came through its use of specific musical conventions and aesthetic features that accompanied the jump in scale, ensuring a smooth landing.

'What A Wonderful World' is based on a chord progression that for the most part conforms to the basic rules of modal or diatonic theory. (It is necessary to briefly summarise some basic premises of modal music here—sometimes treated almost as universal rules of composition—although I intend to denaturalise these premises and rules in the next chapter.) Simply put, Louis Armstrong's version of 'What a Wonderful World' is based on the F major scale, which includes the pitches F, G, A, B♭, C, D, and E. This means F major functions as the 'tonic' chord. (Note that in music theory the term 'global tonic' is sometimes used to describe the key that defines a piece of music as a whole, as opposed to a 'local tonic' which is involved when the piece modulates temporarily to a different key.) According to the conventions of diatonic tonality, listeners experience varying degrees of tension when the chords—always staying within the key—move away from the tonic. They then hear a kind of satisfying resolution when the piece of music returns to that tonic chord. In 'What a Wonderful World', all the opening chords are within the F major key, and the vocal melody initially uses only these notes. The F major chord accompanies the first line ('I see trees …') and the simple observations about the blooming red roses have a broadly conventional accompaniment within the key, following a chord progression that moves through varying kinds of distance from the tonic, but always with the expectation that it will ultimately return to F major and offer some kind of closure.

However, something different happens towards the end of the verse, exactly when the lyrics jump from these specific observations ('I see them bloom') to general claim ('what a wonderful world'). The line 'and I think to myself' is accompanied by a transition to a chord that is *not* in the F major key. This is the D flat major seven chord, which includes several pitches *not* in the F major scale (although it does include the pitches of F and C). The chord therefore sounds strange, not fundamentally wrong but ambiguous, unsettling, a step outside expectations. This type of chord is often known as a tritone substitution.[1] Tritone substitution chords are widely used by jazz musicians to create a sense of uncertainty, intrigue or ambiguity. They may also feature in other popular music genres for a similar purpose. Some of the suggestive, funky, mildly jarring chords that Stevie Wonder uses, for example, are also tritone substitutions. So, as Armstrong sings 'think to myself …', the accompanying chord sounds strange, unsettled or uncertain to listeners who are in some sense familiar with the conventions of Western music, or who have a sense of the key the song is in. It creates a strong feeling of distance from the tonic chord, along with a kind of ambiguity or doubt. Unlike other chords within the key, it does not come with the assurance of resolution. It could be inaugurating a key change, in fact. (In 'What a Wonderful World', it could signify a shift to the parallel key of F minor, for example.) The fact of it being a temporary substitution from the chords in the key is only confirmed when the piece returns to chords in the original key.

This tritone substitution chord is emphasised in Armstrong's 'What a Wonderful World' in three main ways. First, as the chord changes, the pitch of the vocal melody does not. That is, the singer reaches the pitch of F at the word 'you' in 'for me and you' then stays on it through the following 'and I think to myself what a', so the chord change (at 'think') is the only thing that changes harmonically. This makes the chord transition more noticeable. (The vocal melody staying on the same note for so long also contributes to the sense of the song balancing uncertainly, unsure of which way to go.) Second, at the transition to the tritone substitution chord, several instruments temporarily drop out. The verse is accompanied by arpeggios on the guitar and by smooth strings, but the strings disappear as Armstrong sings 'and I think to myself'. This dropping of a key part of the instrumental accompaniment creates a temporarily stark or spare musical texture that emphasises the remaining elements (namely, the guitar's move to the tritone substitution chord). And third, the chord is emphasised by the fact that it lasts twice as long as the preceding chords in

[1] In music-theoretical terms, a musician is playing a tritone substitution when they play a dominant seventh chord that is a tritone away from a dominant seventh chord in a key. It works—it does not sound completely out of key or out of place but instead adds an intriguing flavour or tension—because the two chords share the same tritone interval. Although the 'What a Wonderful World' chord described above is an unconventional example of a tritone substitution and may not qualify as one according to some interpretations of jazz music theory, I nevertheless retain the term here, partly for the sake of having a simple term to use for the crucial chord.

the verse. A stable, consistent momentum builds in the introduction and the verse with a chord change every two beats (i.e. two chords per bar). Then, the sustained tritone substitution chord is the first time the chord lasts a full bar. This longer chord gives a sense of suspended momentum, reinforcing the feeling of uncertainty. Lekman emphasised this even further in his performance by prolonging the chord, letting it ring out beyond the end of the bar and into silence, temporarily losing strict time before finally resuming with the key line: 'what a wonderful world'.

And this is surely the key line: the scale-jumping or transition to 'Whole-World thinking' (Glissant, 2020) is only complete with the word 'world'. The line could have been 'what a wonderful park', 'what a wonderful day', 'what a wonderful sight', 'what a wonderful town', 'what a wonderful garden' or 'what a wonderful place'. Each of these would have been a more *reasonable* statement to make after the series of specific observations of trees and flowers, but instead it is specifically a wonderful *world*.

So, if the sense of taking a leap is supported by the ambiguity and uncertainty of the suspended tritone substitution chord, how does the music *land the jump*? How does it finally achieve this transition?

It does so partly through a reassuring and familiar cadence (i.e. the resolution of the musical phrase) in the chords. The chords move from C7 to F (the 'dominant' chord to the 'root' chord of the key) in a 'perfect' or 'authentic' cadence that lands back at the tonic. This is an extremely common cadence in Western popular music, especially at the ending of a section or song, and it is associated with a strong sense of satisfying resolution or closure. The transition from C7 to F is especially satisfying because of smooth 'voice leading' whereby the seventh of C7 (which is Bb) moves down a semitone to the third of F (which is A). The effect of this closure in 'What a Wonderful World' is doubly strong after the radical uncertainty of the tritone chord. To reach the home or tonic chord via the most familiar-sounding cadence resolves all the tension in the most smooth and resounding way possible. Crucially, this return to the tonic in the chords happens just as Armstrong sings the word 'world'. The sense of having leaped uncertainly that was generated with the extended tritone substitution chord is resolved, such that musically the song makes landing on the word 'world' seem pretty much as natural and satisfying as is possible within the conventions of modern Western music.

There is one more point to add to this, though. Armstrong could have increased or reinforced the sense of closure and resolution even more by also singing 'world' on the pitch of F, but—the first time, at least—he does not. The first time he sings 'what a wonderful world', the melody moves from F ('what a'), down to E ('won'), then smoothly upwards: F ('der'), G ('ful'), A ('world'). It would have been perfectly natural, indeed conventional, to end back down at F in the vocal melody, but the move to A gives some sense of upward motion, of having arrived somewhere other than where he started. The end on A sounds pleasing in part because of the aforementioned 'voice leading' in the chords (i.e. the move from C7 to F entailing the half-tone move down from Bb to A), but it still gives a greater sense of uplift, and of having reached somewhere new, than the more conventionally reassuring return to F. (In fact, the last time Armstrong sings 'what a wonderful world', the 'world' does land on F, giving some finality to the song.)

If these details sound overly technical, just listen to the song from the beginning, and pay attention to how the chord sounds at 'think to myself' (0:21–0:24), and the effect of the higher-pitched note at 'world' (0:27–0:28), and hopefully the basic point will be discernible: there is a moment of ambiguity at 'think to myself', and sense of closure as well as upward movement at 'world'. I suggest that all this can be understood as musical scale-jumping, or the artistic and aesthetic relation of the local particulars in the verse to the general claim of the world being wonderful.

These specific features of 'What a Wonderful World'—the tritone substitution chord, the perfect cadence and so on—are just some of the many composition techniques and performance and production details musicians use to create some sense of transition or breakthrough from one mood or state to another, often at the transition between different structural elements of a piece (e.g. between verse and chorus, and back again). A famous one is the key change, which featured in around a quarter of pop hits in the second half of the twentieth century, often to build additional energy at the closing chorus. Listen, for example, to 03:23 in Bon Jovi's 'Living on a Prayer' (1986) to hear this musical method of breaking through to a higher level. In the rock tradition, drummers commonly vary the dynamics of their performance to introduce new sections, through loosening the hi-hat or providing drum fills as a chorus approaches. Rock guitarists change their playing style or employ an effects pedal at transitional moments in songs, too. In the twenty-first century, many contemporary EDM-inspired pop songs favour timbre-based production techniques such as 'drops' and filter sweeps for similar transition purposes. These can often build tension, create a moment of crisis and thereby increase the intensity or emphasis on the release or resolution of that

tension. All these kinds of techniques could be used to accompany a similar lyrical leap from the specific to the general; many of them feature, in
fact, at the moment when both Tears for Fears (1982) and Gary Jules
(2001) declare, on the basis of their personal experience, that 'it's a very
very mad world'. In both versions of 'Mad World', there are several strik-
ing tonal, dynamics and production changes as the chorus reaches its key
claim. Indeed, many songs achieve this kind of jump in scale, and the
techniques described for Armstrong's 'What a Wonderful World' are far
from the only musical methods of scale-jumping available.

Furthermore, the techniques in Armstrong's version are not always
used to the same scale-jumping effect, nor are they applied consistently by
everyone who performs it. Jens Lekman, for example, adapted the song in
ways that specifically highlighted the scale-jumping effect and its political
implications in the Lysekil context of counterposing 'six hundred jobs'
with 'life on Earth'. His version was transposed into the key of E major,
and Lekman sang the melody almost an octave higher than in Armstrong's
original. His higher-pitched voice, with its characteristic naivety, sensitivity
and vulnerability, made the song sound sadder, as if lamenting what could
be lost (rather than, as in Armstrong's version, celebrating the beauty of
the world). Lekman's live version also replaced the original's lush, rich,
full instrumentation with a simple acoustic guitar accompaniment, producing a sparer, more stripped-down texture that emphasised the vulnerability of his voice. Whereas the guitar in Armstrong's version plays
arpeggios (i.e. individually picked strings playing each note of the chord in
sequence), Lekman kept the same metre but with full strummed chords
(i.e. all the strings played simultaneously). This had the effect of making
the moment of transition to the tritone substitution chord more immediately noticeable. And in this section of the original version, Armstrong
sings 'wonderful world' as a full, smooth phrase with no pause, but
Lekman left a noticeable gap separating 'wonderful' from 'world', prolonging the sense of uncertainty and delaying the closure of the final line,
perhaps with the intention of stressing that scalar jump. This separation
was even clearer the final time, as Lekman also let the guitar ring silent
during a long pause, before finally reaching 'world' on the tonic. All these
adaptations brought the radical and, in this context, politically vital leap to
'Whole-World thinking' to the fore.

With the exception of this adaptation, Lekman stayed closely to the
precise rhythm of the vocal melody, even more so than Armstrong, who
came from a jazz tradition. But other versions of the song have been much

more relaxed and playful in this respect. Another famous version was recorded by Tony Bennett and k.d. lang in 2002 for an album of classics entitled 'A Wonderful World'. In their version of 'What a Wonderful World', they demonstrate what Allan Moore (2012, 103) would describe as an 'extremely laid back' 'heard attitude to rhythm', with an almost conversational style in the duet. This means that they intentionally do not sing in time with the beat; sometimes they leave long pauses after the chord change before essentially catching up, at their own speed. This unhurried attitude with a varying rhythm in the vocal melody is just one of a series of features in this version that emphasises the mysterious, woozy, dream-like and even magical elements of the song. In k.d. lang's first verse, there is minimal percussion and the beat is not prominent, which makes it sound less rigidly structured. Then, at the transition to the tritone substitution chord, we hear the prominent ring of a single note probably on a vibraphone or other metallophone instrument. This is the kind of sound, often provided by a tinkling triangle or resonant bell, that might accompany a moment of 'magic' in a classic Hollywood movie. In this version of 'What a Wonderful World', in the context of the more woozy rhythm and atmosphere, it makes that moment of scale-jumping sound distinctly 'magical'.

Another famous recording of the song is by Joey Ramone's, also from 2002. This is radically different in a rhythmic sense from Armstrong's, Bennet and lang's and Lekman's versions, with its various musical features from the rock tradition emphasising not a 'magic' leap per se but, rather, a moment of radical *breakthrough* to a new level. It replaces the arpeggios on the acoustic guitar with bar chords on an electric guitar playing eight strums per beat, which makes the song sound extremely different metrically and dynamically. Ramone sings with a much stricter 'attitude to rhythm' (Moore, 2012, 103); his more staccato vocals are perfectly in time with the beat. It is also faster, with its steadier, simple rhythm creating greater urgency and a more unstoppable, train-like momentum. The scale-jump is emphasised by different kinds of dynamic features: most notably, the guitar is palm-muted in the verse accompaniment in time with the beat but then, at the transition to the tritone substitution chord ('... think to myself ...'), Ramone lets the full, sustained chord ring out. He also adds a lead guitar lick here. This dramatic dynamic change is also heard in the drums, which become more intense at that point, switching from a closed-high-hat sound in the verse to cymbals that are more resonant. These are all techniques commonly heard at moments of transition in rock and grunge songs, and they are perfectly suited in this context to give that sense of breaking through to a new level. Ramone reinforces this euphoric sense of reaching a higher level at the end of the song, too. Whereas Armstrong, Lekman and Bennett and lang all end their versions with a strong sense of closure by singing 'world' on the tonic note, Ramone actually reaches a higher pitch with a different closing melody at this point in his recording. His version resembles Lekman's in the long pause, fading to silence, it leaves for the final 'what a wonderful ...'. Here the drums finally drop out and the song's rhythm is paused for the first time, as if finally suspended mid-jump. But then energy is reinjected for 'world', which moves through a different melody that gives a stronger sense of final uplift than in any of these other versions.

These examples demonstrate the musical scale-jump can be achieved in fundamentally different ways, even in versions of the same composition. In fact, the original can be transformed almost beyond recognition but still put to the same scale-jumping purposes. Watch, for example, the promotional video for 'The Line', an apparently revolutionary proposal for an urban living concept in Saudi Arabia, described as a 'linear smart city'.[2] The video begins with a depiction of a woman in a grey, banal, everyday urban scene. She then jumps through a kind of portal that transports her into a radically futuristic, bright and colourful vision of life in 'The Line'. The soundtrack to this is a shortened and transformed version of 'What a Wonderful World' with an entirely different chord structure. The 'red roses too ... think to myself' lines accompany the opening scenes of urban dullness. Then, a combination of dynamic changes accompany the singer's 'what a wonderful ...' as the depicted woman jumps through the portal. At 'world', the musical style has transformed dramatically, as the woman explores this new and revolutionary world of urban living. There is no tritone substitution chord here, nor do we hear the melody or cadences of the original and its famous cover versions. These features are replaced with filters and other production techniques from the EDM tradition that achieve by other means a similarly radical sense of finding a new level or of breaking through to the other side of a boundary, just as we hear the words 'what a wonderful world' for the first time. It may be significant, nonetheless, that those promoting 'The Line' chose 'What a Wonderful World' for the marketing campaign. Even in its radically altered form, its

<hr>

[2] On YouTube, the video is entitled 'NEOM | THE LINE—New Wonders for the World'. It was posted by NEOM on 22 July 2022 and by March 2023 it had been viewed 50 million times.

associations with breaking through, with moving beyond the banal and reaching a higher plane of reality, still function.

Other performances of the song have even minimised or entirely abrogated its scale-jumping function, for different reasons and in different ways. Dwayne 'The Rock' Johnson performed a version for Michael Caine and Josh Hutcherson's characters in the 2012 movie 'Journey 2: The Mysterious Island'. Johnson also sang in a version recorded for the opening credits. This has different verse lyrics and a much faster dance rhythm, with no dynamic change at all at the tritone substitution chord. The only sense of 'breakthrough' occurs in an additional instrumental section at the end, which features an upward key change. It seems to have been conceived as a generally uplifting song about the world's wonderfulness, with no need to express the same jump from the particular to the general. The original Armstrong version features in a similarly flat sense but with a different purpose in the opening scenes of another movie: 'Good Morning, Vietnam' (1987). In that case, the song soundtracks montaged shots of violence and poverty in the Vietnam War, after being introduced on the radio by the disc jockey Adrian Cronauer (played by Robin Williams). In this context it features in a darkly ironic register, with the positive claim of it being 'a wonderful world' clashing uncomfortably with the scenes depicted. This ironic message also came through in a solo pianist's performance of 'What a Wonderful World' outside a railway station in Lviv, Ukraine, in March 2022. A video of this performance was widely shared on social media, and it shows the pianist playing an instrumental version that, in the context of the fear and displacement caused by Russia's invasion of Ukraine in February 2022, registers as bleakly, darkly ironic.[3] This version is transposed into the key of A major and played at a faster pace than Armstrong's and especially Bennett and lang's versions, with none of the uplifting or magical atmosphere. The pianist plays the chords as light arpeggios in the verse section, but at the transition to the tritone substitution, she switches to a full chord with a prominent bass, such that any lightness is quickly dispelled. Besides this, there is no dynamic change at this point, as this performance seems not to be concerned with jumping scale but, rather, with a general expression of dark, tragic irony. The bass-heavy chord on a slightly out-of-tune piano does, however, make the 'think to myself' section sound particularly dissonant, discordant and dark.

---

[3] See the video posted on Twitter by Andrew RC Marshall [@Journotopia], 5 March 2022.

So, even if 'What a Wonderful World' functions as a scale-jumping song, especially in the context in which Jens Lekman performed it, emphasising and extending many of the original recording's key musical scale-jumping features, the song does not always achieve this jump in scale. This point testifies to more than merely the remarkably flexible, context-dependent and endlessly reinterpretable nature of the popular song. It indicates something about the nature of musical scale-jumping and of the cultural production of scale more generally.

The artistic connection of local, discrete, personal experience and general truth is long-established, such that this leap does not need to be made every time. Even within 'What a Wonderful World', it is surely the first verse, or the first tritone-substitution-and-perfect-cadence, that really makes the jump; the rest of the song normalises and naturalises it through repetition and variation on the same theme. It is also fair to say that the overall effect of the song is not to draw attention to the jump per se, as if it is showing the cleverness of its own ability to make that jump. Instead of making the jump seem remarkable, the song's functioning relies on a cultural convention in which the *connectedness* or *inseparability* of the personal and the general, the local and the world, the particular and the universal, is already established and naturalised, in the history of music and in arts and culture more generally. 'What a Wonderful World' has been part of establishing this, but it is just one of endless examples that have had this kind of accretional, long-term effect on people's expectations of how culture produces and navigates scale. Cultural practices have long moved smoothly between these local and general poles, with the effect of establishing a naturalised relation between them, or even of fusing or entirely eliding the distinction.

For Glissant, this is the essential vocation of the artist or poet: to 'establish Relation', or to trace, beat and re-trace 'the path that leads from our place to the world and back again' (Glissant, 2020, 73; 118). It is through culture that we 'discover that the place we live in, that we speak from, can no longer be separated from this mass of energy that calls us in the distance. We can no longer grasp its movement, its infinite variations, its sufferings and its pleasures, unless we relate it to that which moves so totally for us, in the totality of the world' (ibid., 73). Simply put: 'To write is to say: the world' (ibid.). We are all, always, all of us, working with the 'intertwined poetics that allow me to sense how my place joins up with others' (ibid., 74). None of us can help but hear the 'unstoppable murmuring' of the world and we all 'mix [it] into the mechanical, humdrum little tunes of our progress and our driftings' (ibid., 8). The Whole-World, the rhizomatic totality, 'demands our attention more every day and we are obliged to test our abilities against it. The writer and the artists have asked us to do this. Their work is marked by this vocation' (ibid., 106). Further:

> Everyone is embarking, at every moment, on a Treatise on the Whole-World. There are a hundred thousand billions of them, rising up every-where. Each time different in sea spray and soil. In Guadeloupe or Valparaiso, you leave from Baffin Island, or the land of Sumatra or the bungalow *Mon repos*, first turning after the Post Office, or, if your silt has crumbled around you, from a line that you have sketched out in the spaces, and you rise to that knowledge. (Ibid., 109)

Crucially, this is not, for Glissant, a generalising or universalising practice. Quite the opposite. The kind of 'Whole-World thinking' we find in differ-ent cultural forms is concerned with 'the rhizome of all places that makes up the totality' and with 'the infinite detail of the real' (ibid., 109; 118). It is a concern with the world's 'extraordinary hybridity… the actual sub-stance of each of their places, their minute or infinite detail and the thrill-ing sum of their particularities, that is to be placed in complicity with those of all places' (ibid., 73). Glissant attends to those cultural practices that trace what Celia Britton (in ibid., 2) calls 'an important and non-conflictual relation between the specificity of the place that one lives in and the world in general'. It is 'trace thought', as opposed to 'systematic thought', that puts our place in relation and 'sings its relativity' (ibid., 50). This *trace* 'puts us, all of us, wherever we come from, in Relation' (ibid., 9). His 'Poetics of Relation' is what 'leads us to conceive of the elusive "world-ness"' of the 'piling up of flashes of light, of communications', 'at the same time as it allows us to pick up some detail from it, and in particular to sing the praises of our place, unfathomable and irreversible' (ibid., 12; 101). So, while Smith (1996) focuses on the practical 'scale-jumping' function of cultural artefacts, Glissant's 'Whole-World thinking' leads us instead to emphasise the scalar work of art *as* art and, to some extent, to judge art by its scale-jumping function.

As this chapter has shown, 'What a Wonderful World' is a piece of music that can have a kind of scale-jumping function in specific contexts. At the climate protest, it changed the scalar politics of the day, musically recasting the scale of the political struggle from 'six hundred jobs' in Lysekil to 'life on Earth'. But it did not do so through some narrowly practical applica-tion; its effectiveness came through its cultural performance and through its qualities as music—or at least through its manipulation of a pre-existing set of cultural expectations about musical resolution to a tonic, and through its subtle compositional features that accompany a natural and satisfying transition from the particular to the general. It is a song that traces and makes interrelations through a kind of poetic 'wandering', and through playing with 'conjunctions of forms and structures that allow an idea of the world' (Glissant, 2020, 19), as well as the 'fractures and ruptures' that fuse and lead to new relations and 'completely new outcomes' (ibid., 13–14). Simply put, it does not so much jump scales as trace the path or fuse a new relation between the particular and the general, between this place and a common, shared Whole-World, or the local-experiential and the general. It produces, in some sense, a flattened scalar system in which the local and the global, say, cannot be abstracted from or used to explain the other; instead, they are part of the same continuum or category. Music is one of those artistic and poetic forms that somehow 'preserves' or brings to rest the infinite 'piling up of flashes of light, of communications' that we otherwise naively and disjointedly experience as the Whole-World (ibid., 100; 101). Music is, by extension, one of those cultural forms that enable certain kinds of truth claims about the world— truth claims taken to be useful, valid, shareable, compelling; that it is wonderful, for example—that are not based on stably replicable scientific procedures or evidence. It has features and functions that make such claims work in persuasive ways and with political and practical effects. Through music, moreover, scalar jumps become normalised and stabilised as new relations, such that they no longer register notably as 'jumps'. Instead, they fuse connections that become common-sense. As Glissant (2020, 108) puts it, 'we are no longer able to sing, speak or work based on our place alone, without plunging into the imagination of this totality'. We already live in a world whose scales are made by music.

References

Dodds, P. (2019). Hearing histories of Hammer Hill: Pop music as auditory geography. *Emotion, Space and Society, 30*, 34–40.

Dodds, P. (2021). The new geographies of popular music (in a pandemic): Guilty geographies and compressed intimacies. *POPULÄR – Nordic Journal for Popular Culture Research, 1*(2), 9–27.

Glissant, É. (2020). *Treatise on the Whole-World* (C. Britton, Trans.). Liverpool University Press.

Mitchell, D. (2002). Controlling space, controlling scale: Migratory labour, free speech, and regional development in the American West. *Journal of Historical Geography, 28*(1), 63–84.

Moore, A. (2012). *Song means: Analysing and interpreting recorded popular song*. Ashgate.

Smith, N. (1996). Spaces of vulnerability: The space of flows and the politics of scale. *Critique of Anthropology, 16*(1), 63–77.

CHAPTER 5

The Cultural Production of Scalability: Music, Colonialism and the Moravian Missionary Project

Abstract Analysis of the work of the music historian, composer, editor and Moravian missionary administrator Christian Ignatius Latrobe (1756–1836) enables a better understanding of the role of music in colonial expansion in the first half of the nineteenth century. In London, Latrobe received and circulated accounts of the missions' supposed success in training disciplined and 'sweet' choirs of Christian singers from among formerly 'heathen' 'barbarians', and these accounts were taken to demonstrate the scalability of the 'civilisation' project of European colonialism, which suited both antislavery campaigners and colonial state officials. Latrobe sent standardised Christian hymn books, in English and German but also translated into indigenous languages, to mission stations around the world, from Suriname to Jamaica to Labrador to Greenland to Siberia to South Africa. He also sent musical instruments to accompany the hymn-singing, favouring the organ both aesthetically and for its ability to function in different climates. He also circulated specific instructions for training organists, with firm recommendations for a simple accompaniment style and learning hymns by heart. At the different stations, the policy increasingly became to train local members of the congregation according to Latrobe's advice, so that the instrument, the canon of tunes and the performance conventions were exported uniformly from Europe, embodied in the organ and the organist. Crucially, this uniform and standardised imposition of music—although always resisted and never fully

© The Author(s) 2023
P. Dodds, *Music and the Cultural Production of Scale*,
https://doi.org/10.1007/978-3-031-36283-5_5

achieved—required the remaking of the cultural landscapes on which they were to be imposed, including through the violent outlawing of existing musical practices and styles. As such, key periods in the history of large-scale musical colonisation can be better understood when framed in terms of the cultural production of scalability, following Anna Tsing, with empirical attention to the efforts involved in musical scale-building projects that make claims about music's universal qualities and that seek to propagate a standardised, common music around the world.

Keywords Musical colonisation • Cultural imperialism • Scalability • Universalism • Moravian Church • Missionary music • Christian Ignatius Latrobe • South Africa • Hymn • Organ • Greenland

Listen to:
Come, Holy Ghost, Come, Lord, Our God
The Lord Has Done Great Things For Us

For Édouard Glissant, 'the rhizome of all places that makes up the totality' must be contrasted with what he criticises as 'the temptation of the generalizing universal' (Glissant, 2020, 109; 79). The 'weave' of the world's particularities cannot be treated as 'a generality giving birth to its own generalizations', and he cautions against 'the false clarity of universal models' (ibid., 118; 16). He criticises not the attempt to understand a shared world but the 'imposing' or 'project[ing] into elsewhere' of 'the Universal' (ibid., 61; 37). He asks:

> Why has the rationality of the Universal become the precious and semi-exclusive claim of this collection of cultures that has been called the West? (Ibid., 61)

Scholars have asked this question, especially in the last half century or so, in terms of 'cultural imperialism' (see Tomlinson, 1991), including in the field of music studies (e.g. Garofalo, 1993). The question has been some version of: why has this aspect of culture, or this aspect of music, been somehow imposed beyond its original context such that it now is treated as some kind of universal standard or norm? The title of Geoffrey Baker's (2008) book *Imposing Harmony* on colonial Cusco indicates the trend well. Studies such as Glenda Goodman's (2012) account of 'the Soundscape of Colonialism' in seventeenth-century North America have shown that cultural-imperialist projects in general, and musical colonisation in particular, have a long history. These projects have also always been resisted, very often through indigenous and oppressed groups challenging the universalist premises of cultural or specifically musical imperialism, as much recent work has shown (see, e.g., Okigbo, 2010; Goodman, 2012; Chikowero, 2015; Eyerly, 2020; Ryan, 2021). What Zine Magubane (2004, 148) calls 'the politics of refusal' have been deployed to refuse, re-use, re-appropriate, re-work or otherwise counter the colonial imposition of music, or the imposition of colonial force *through* music. Nevertheless, Dylan Robinson has shown that the 'epistemic violence' of cultural imperialism has had a lasting legacy as a structural feature of settler colonial states, and that it has involved undermining indigenous norms and beliefs about what music is and what it can or should do (Robinson, 2020, 46). Colonialism, for Robinson (ibid., 10), is a 'state of perception'. It applies, as Magubane (2004, 33; 35) points out, an 'Aesthetics of Rule' through the 'fiction of a universal standard of taste'. This Aesthetics of Rule positions racialised and gendered Others as 'objects of aesthetic contemplation' in relation to the gentlemanly 'aesthetic subject' who is constructed as the universal or 'generic perceiver' (ibid., 34). In missionary diaries and travel accounts, for example, 'the one who can see and appreciate beauty is the one who can exercise the right to rule over all those who are merely aesthetic objects' (ibid., 36).

Sarah Justina Eyerly (2020) is one of several scholars who have focused their attention on the particular role of missionaries in musical colonisation. Missionary projects of various kinds 'often equated or presaged acts of cultural genocide' (Eyerly, 2020, 14). Any exceptional 'good' missionaries and their empowering effects on their indigenous congregations notwithstanding, the missionary projects' 'religious soundscapes, and their attendant hymn traditions, can be understood as colonial structures that attempted to standardize, indeed to colonize, indigenous soundscapes, musical practices, and religious traditions' (ibid., 13; see also Chikowero, 2015; Johnson-Williams, 2020). Mhoze Chikowero emphasises how, in the nineteenth- and twentieth-century Zimbabwean context, missionaries 'maligned the power of African song' as part of a 'mission to culturally alienate and disarm' (Chikowero, 2015, 3). European colonialism was 'culturally propagated' through missionaries' use of music 'as a weapon to undermine African sovereignty' (ibid., 2). European colonialism's successful 'propagation' relied on a concerted project of 'epistemicide' whereby 'missionaries cast African musical cultures as paganism, to be destroyed if the African was to be saved' (ibid., 3–4). Grant Olwage (2004; see also 2010) in fact traces 'the Birth of Musical Colonialism' to the large-scale missionary projects in southern Africa in the second half of the nineteenth century. In the examples he focuses on, the musical-colonisers were particularly keen to validate their efforts through 'recurring appeals to "nature"' and to the universal (Olwage, 2010, 196). John Curwen (1816–1880), who diffused the tonic sol-fa system of music education, wrote articles with titles like 'The Musical Scale of All Nations and of All Times' and 'was eulogized as "the father of Universal song"' (ibid., 204). And Olwage argues that the 'theoretical project to universalize sol-fa … speaks also of its universalizing imperialist intentions' (ibid.). Crucially, in these and other accounts, music did not just happen to accompany colonisation, nor even to facilitate or enable it, but it was rather one of the key, indispensable means of large-scale colonial expansion. European Christian hymns were vital in the breaking of new ground, the establishment of new settlements, and the imposition of Western culture, as well as universalised Western norms of aesthetic appreciation and cultural practice, around the world.

For Chikowero (2015, 9), 'Scholars have yet to sufficiently engage with the meaning of the missionary effect on African music'. This point has been made more forcefully in Kofi Agawu's chapter in *Audible Empire* entitled 'Tonality as a Colonizing Force in Africa'. There Agawu assesses how African music was transformed by the imposition of European tonality from the mid-nineteenth century in what amounted 'to musical violence of a very high order, a violence whose psychic and psychological impacts remain to be properly explored' (Agawu, 2016, 338). He argues:

[I]n domesticating hymns whose texts were originally in German or English for local consumption, melodies often disregarded the natural declamation of indigenous singing, imposed a regime of regular and symmetrical periodicity, and rode roughshod over the intonational contours prescribed by speech tones. (Ibid., 338)

Agawu aims to provide 'a step toward future theorization of the dynamics of musical colonization' but regrets that musical colonisation remains understudied (ibid.).

Here I want to suggest a further step in understanding the dynamics of musical colonisation by attending to the *production of scalability* in relation to Moravian missionaries' musical methods in the early part of the nineteenth century, including in Africa, but before the period that Agawu, Olwage, Chikowero and others have focused on. I likewise propose to analyse the efforts to make 'universal' claims about music, as this was a crucial part of the moral justification and implied effectiveness of the Moravians' musical strategies. To universalise (in the Glissantian sense of imposing or projecting) something like music is not easy; it takes effort. Specifically, it takes what Anna Tsing (2012) calls 'scale-building' effort and 'scalability projects'.

Tsing explains that scalable projects are those that have 'the ability to expand—and expand, and expand—without rethinking basic elements' (ibid., 143). Scalability 'block[s] our ability to notice the heterogeneity of the world' and 'allows us to see only uniform blocks, ready for further expansion' (ibid.). To achieve scalability, the essential project elements must not form 'transformative relationships [which] are the medium for the emergence of diversity ... that might change things' (ibid., 145). For this reason, Tsing uses the logic and language of the 'pixel' to describe the production of 'uniform, separate, and autonomous' units 'cleansed of transformative social relations' (ibid., 146; 151). These pixel-like interchangeable, zoomable units are what scalability thrives on. So when Garofalo (1993, 26), for example, explains the global success of rock music in terms of it being 'easy to export', 'easy to indigenize' and 'readily amenable to local content' with 'stylistic elements which can easily be incorporated into local musics', he is describing the essential scalability of rock music: that it does not need to be transformed to be applied at a large scale. Will Straw (1991, 378) similarly explains how the 'localism' of alternative rock 'has been reproduced, in relatively uniform ways, on a continental and international level', and in doing so he also makes a scalability argument:

> The ability of groups and records to circulate from one local scene to another, in a manner that requires little in the way of adaptation to local circumstances, is an index of the way in which a particularly stable set of musical languages and relationships between them has been reproduced within a variety of local circumstances. (Ibid., 379)

The critical thrust of Straw's and Garofalo's observations is that this globalised music system means obsolescence for those who do not adopt the scalable template or model. What they both miss is a Tsingian perspective of how these sets of 'locals' that are amenable to the globally circulating, exportable forms have themselves been *made* as part of the scalability project: it was not just that a few musicians worked out how to make music that would work at scale; they relied on and in some cases contributed to bigger, pre-existing and ongoing scale-making efforts that produced the pixel-like set of locals to which their music was amenable. This is the essential insight of Tsing (2005, 57): 'projects cannot limit themselves to conjuring at different scales—they must conjure the scales themselves.' They must also produce scalability.

So, when it comes to the Moravian missionaries' musical scale-conjuring, there is only one man to start with: Christian Ignatius Latrobe (1758–1836). As the London-based administrator of Moravian mission work, Latrobe sat at the very centre of a Latourian 'centre of calculation' where 'masses of inscriptions pour in, tipping the *scale* once again by forcing the world to come to the centres' (Latour, 1987, 233; italics in original). For a half-century, from the 1780s to the 1830s, it was his job as Secretary of the Church and Missions of the United Brethren to correspond with Moravian missionaries stationed in Greenland, Canada, the US, the West Indies, Suriname, Siberia, South Africa and several other missions of varying size and success around the world. His archived correspondence in the Moravian Church Archives in London is organised into sections for, say, Tobago, Labrador and the Calmucks, and his private journal in Manchester's John Rylands Library describes his daily work engaging with these varied communications. Based in the department for the 'Superintendency of the Missions', his job was essentially to administer and oversee the whole Moravian project:

> All Missionaries keep up a constant correspondence with this department, and also transmit to them copies of their Diaries and Journals. A Secretary is appointed to make extracts from them, of which manuscript copies are sent and read to all the congregations and Missions. (PA VII 1819–20, 16)

Indeed, he was also tasked with circulating the correspondence that came to him in London back out to all the missions, and he did this partly by editing a regular publication of *Periodical Accounts of the Church of the*

United Brethren that he then posted around the world.[1] This enabled the missions to feel part of a global effort and, importantly, to share when certain methods had succeeded. Through this circulating correspondence Latrobe could help build and share a standardised, best-practice model of missionary behaviour. And besides the paperwork, it was Latrobe's job to source and send the items necessary for missionary success around the world. He sent maps, tools, bells and building materials, but the most common items requested by the missionaries and sent by Latrobe were hymn books. He also took a keen interest in the musical instruments that would be used in the missionaries' religious services. The *Periodical Accounts* contain several mentions of missionaries receiving with gratitude musical instruments that had been sent by Latrobe in London. (The ship that delivered a violincello to Labrador, for example, was called 'the Harmony'.) Latrobe's diary also shows that he helped new missionaries pack and prepare for their trips out into the field, and this often involved helping them pick out the best lightweight, mobile musical instruments.

Latrobe's personal network in Europe included music historians such as Charles Burney as well as some of the leading musicians of the day, especially Joseph Haydn, who was Latrobe's favourite. Latrobe himself was influential in his time as a composer and especially as an editor of collections of hymns and sacred music. In 1790 Latrobe edited the first English edition of Moravian hymn tunes, including around a dozen of his own compositions. That hymn book and its subsequent editions continued to be used by missionaries throughout the nineteenth century. Latrobe's passion was music, which he saw as both spiritually and practically crucial for the evangelical cause. He wrote, in 1815, on his return from an official visit to the missions in South Africa:

> Among the precious gifts which it has pleased God to bestow upon his creature man ... I consider *music* as one of the most important and valuable, both as to its nature, its effects, its use, and its eternal duration. (Latrobe's letter to his daughter Agnes, quoted in *The Moravian Church Miscellany* IV 1853, 345; italics in original)

He emphasised both 'the secret and mysterious power which it possesses over the heart, and the rapturous delight which it conveys to the

---

[1] The various volumes of the *Periodical Accounts* are cited here as: 'PA [volume number] [dates of publication]'.

intellectual part of man, and which language cannot describe' (ibid., 345–6). He recorded in his diary the many debates and discussions he had among his friends about the use and potential misuse of something with such power over the heart and mind, but he always returned to his unwavering belief that religious messages could be 'brought home to the heart by Verse easier than Prose' (Journal of Christian Ignatius Latrobe, 9 Jan 1788, f. 2; underlines in original).

This belief that music should be used for delivering and supporting clear spiritual messages meant that he favoured certain musical features. For hymns he favoured a homophonic melody with a separate note for each syllable to increase clarity, and he strongly advocated a restrained and sober accompaniment style, ideally on an organ. He criticised flourishes and unnecessary ornaments in the musical accompaniment, as they would distract from the words and their meaning. He spent several years deriding what he saw as an overly demonstrative organ-playing style and the tendency to play 'jiggish' tunes in church and at other denominations' mission stations (Latrobe, 1818, 216). Instead, he promoted a slow, steady, sober approach to accompaniment with an emphasis on 'Correctness and *Simplicity*, the two grand sources of beauty in the performance of Music' (Latrobe, 1828 I, 2–3; italics in original). He thought that flourishes and fast transitions would distract from the spiritual messages and also make it impossible for a large congregation of untrained singers to follow. Even more complex anthems should not be 'disfigured by slurs, passing notes, and flourishing interludes' (ibid., iv). In fact, Latrobe was the key figure in a stylistic revolution in Moravian church music, instituting a simplified accompaniment style that Moravian missionaries continued to use through the next two centuries (Stevens, 1971). Of course, this standardisation of a simpler form of accompaniment that did not require advanced musical skills made these Moravian hymn performances more scalable, that is, reproducible in contexts even where virtuosos were unavailable.

Through his position at the administrative centre of the Moravian missionary project, Latrobe contributed to the institution of a large-scale, standardised mission model. He received all the different missions' reports, diaries and correspondence, sending back advice and materials, and he published edited selections of these in the *Periodical Accounts*, which he also sent back around the different missions. Many of the letters he received from the different missionaries begin by thanking Latrobe for having sent the latest editions of the *Periodical Accounts* with news of Moravian progress. Some of the missionaries also mention that they read these texts aloud to their assembled congregations. Latrobe edited selectively and inserted his own comments when he wanted to emphasise a point, especially in relation to music. For example, he included an extract of the 1809 diary of the Gnadenthal mission in the Cape Colony describing how the African congregation were apparently 'struck and delighted' by the performance of an anthem by four European missionaries. Latrobe inserted an explanatory footnote: 'Their [the congregation's] surprise was chiefly occasioned by hearing the four natural parts of harmony, each singing to appearance a different tune, and yet all sweetly flowing together in one' (PA V 1811–14, 7). But the primary method of standardising a policy was simply to circulate news of its success. For example, the simplicity of the congregation's singing in Labrador—and the apparently positive effect of this on the congregation's Christian sincerity—was emphasised. Latrobe also drew attention to the Greenland example as a model to follow, not least because of the apparent effectiveness of the formal singing schools that had been instituted before later becoming unnecessary because of communal self-education. In the early editions of the *Periodical Accounts*, Latrobe quoted with approval sections from David Cranz's *History of Greenland* (1767), part of which 'describes very minutely the mode by which the Missionaries proceed among the free Heathen: which indeed is every where the same as to the main point' (PA I 1790–95, 12). Latrobe must have known that the Moravian mission being 'every where the same' was an aim rather than a reality at that point, but he likely wanted to use Cranz's description of the role of music and singing in the missionary project as an example:

> Singing, if sweet, and accompanied with a feeling of heart, is not the smallest part of a rational worship; the hymn-theology being of so much the more blessed tendency, as hymns are easily learnt, and charmingly sung even by the smallest children; and thus all, even the profoundest truths, may, as it were, in a way of refreshment, be insinuated with almost an indelible impression into their minds ... the blessing of which is beyond description, both upon the hearts, and for the advancement of young and old in knowledge. (Cranz, 1767 II, 370)

Latrobe circulated several examples of missionaries using singing and music when making first contact with potential converts around the world. (In the language of the time, these potential converts and established congregations were 'hearers' and/or 'the auditory' who, if they proved unresponsive, were said to be 'not ready to hear'.) It also became clear through the collected reports that the first, most basic and most fundamental task of the missionaries was to translate European, Christian hymns into the language of the people among whom they were working. This was considered the best means of beginning the process of *insinuation*. All this became clear through the correspondence and *Periodical Accounts* that Latrobe maintained.

Hymn translation was usually an extremely difficult task, executed imperfectly and often with disregard for the rhythms, rhymes and intonations of the native languages (see Goodman, 2012; Agawu, 2016), but it was the primary task of the missionary in the field, and it contributed to the global standardisation, or the Glissantian *universalisation*, of music. It was also a task that connected the field missionary to Latrobe in the administrative centre, as he would receive these manuscript translations and arrange for them to be printed in London, before sending them back to the mission stations. (Many of Latrobe's incoming letters acknowledge receipt of these hymn books and thank him for his efforts in printing and posting them.) In general, the missionaries translated hymns from the standard Moravian hymn books, including those compiled and even composed by Latrobe. This meant that when the *Periodical Accounts* described performances of, for example, 'The Lord Has Done Great Things For Us' among the congregations in Greenland and South Africa, Latrobe could insert a standardised hymn number (e.g. 'No 613') and/or page number from the common Moravian hymn book. The *Periodical Accounts* also contained examples of missionaries in Suriname, Greenland and Delaware composing their own hymns, but these compositions followed the established Moravian conventions. There were even examples of what Eyerly calls 'indigenized forms of Christianity and music-making' among the 'Native Christians' who composed their own hymns (Eyerly, 2020, 15), but the fundamentals of Moravian musicking remained. Latrobe hoped, as he wrote in his introduction to his collection of hymn tunes, that the same spiritually uplifting music should be heard 'in all our congregations; and that, scattered as we are in all parts of the world, we may nevertheless, in this part of our worship also, be perfectly uniform' (Latrobe, 1790, ii). His hope that 'pleasing uniformity may … be established among us' in matters of music (ibid.) was part of the Moravian aim to establish themselves as 'one people' who shared a faith, an evangelical mission and a standardised set of cultural practices that could overcome national or tribal differences (see Schutt, 1999).

It is remarkable how much emphasis the Moravians placed on singing and music as evidence of spiritual conversion and of the progress or success of the mission more generally. Missionaries often remarked on their congregations' 'sweet' or 'harmonious' singing 'in unison'. They heard this style of singing as the fruit of their missionary labours, especially when compared with the singing they claimed to have first encountered, which they often described as ugly, inharmonious and muddled. Cranz's *History of Greenland*, for example, contains a missionary's description of overhearing the 'extraordinary sweet singing' of a converted family's morning hymns:

[W]e stood still and listened to this sweet melody with hearts exceedingly moved, and with tears in our eyes … These people were no longer than two years ago savage heathens, and now they sing to the Lamb that was slain, in so sweet a manner, that it penetrates one's marrow and bone. (Cranz, 1767 II, 370)

Often it is the overheard, undirected nature of the singing that provokes such an emotional response. The *Periodical Accounts* contain many such examples of apparently spontaneous Christian song from among the converts being celebrated as evidence of the mission's success. But more formal or coordinated performances were important too. A particular trope was that when missionaries arrived at an established mission station for the first time they would be greeted with a hymn from the assembled congregation, and this musical welcome would be reported as a testament to the mission's progress. It was, for the missionary, remarkable to find people 'seated only a few years ago in darkness, and now singing melodical hymns for the living God' (quoted in Boon, 2015, 73). Latrobe received a letter of this kind from a missionary who had recently arrived at one of the South African mission stations in 1807 and he published it in the *Periodical Accounts*:

My dear Friend! I wish you could waft yourself hither for but eight or ten days. I am pretty sure you would not often have a dry eye, in beholding what the Lord has done for this nation, which but a few years ago was buried in gross ignorance, darkness, and sin: I am not able to describe it, it must be seen and felt. Whenever I hear them sing that verse: '*The Lord for us great things hath done*,' &c. I feel my whole soul melted within me! they [*sic*] do it with such energy and sincere thanksgiving. (PA IV 1806–10, 297–8)

Latrobe received and published further musical evidence of the progress of the South African mission in 1811:

> You may conceive how we felt, while we were sitting at dinner, to hear the voices of the greater part of our congregation, which had assembled unknown to us before our door, singing the praises of our Saviour with cheerful hearts. I assure you, it penetrated our very souls. Thus also, after the close of the evening-service, the whole congregation remained standing before the church, and continued, for a long time, singing hymns of praise and thanksgiving. The evening being very calm, the chorus of … sweet voices seemed to be carried forward through the air, and was echoed back from the hills in a most delightful manner. I wish you could be witness to the effect of such music. The Hottentots never fail to add their favourite hymn, '*The Lord has done great things for us*,' &c. which is, indeed a most heart-reviving truth. (PA V 1811–14, 246)

Latrobe did ultimately hear this for himself. In 1815–16 he took a tour of the South African mission stations, the only such tour he did in his capacity as an overseer of the Moravian missionary project. He was welcomed by the singing of the congregation and he was overwhelmed with joy upon

> seeing this company, lately a scattered race of wretched, ignorant, and wicked heathen, but now brought together as a people of God … Here is seen the effect produced by the preaching of the gospel of a crucified Saviour, unadorned and unaided by human eloquence! I was greatly affected, beyond the power of utterance, and we all stood in silent devotion, listening to the sweet voices, which formed their delightful chorus. (Latrobe, 1818, 40)

For Latrobe, whose job it was also to attract funding from Europeans sympathetic to the cause, these musical descriptions helped demonstrate that the Moravians' missionary efforts were bearing fruit and were therefore worthy of further support. The *Periodical Accounts* also recount many occasions of white Europeans, including colonial governors and officials, visiting the missions and expressing their satisfaction at the quality of the congregations' singing. When some Danish plantation owners travelled over from Demerara to visit the Suriname mission in 1803, they 'expressed their surprize [sic] at the order, stillness, and harmonious singing of the Indian congregation' (PA III 1801–05, 137). In 1804, the South African missions were frequently visited by military officers and Cape Colony officials who were said to be 'delighted with the singing' and 'observed, that it was manifest, that our people sung not with their voices only, but with their hearts' (PA IV 1806–10, 43). Three different Governors of the Cape Colony visited in 1806, 1808 and 1813 respectively, and each apparently declared himself pleasantly surprised at the quality of the singing, and promised his financial and political support for the mission (ibid., 172–4; 368–9).

These performances and their anecdotal retelling fitted into the Moravian strategy of emphasising the quality rather than quantity of converts— Cranz, for example, described his aim as 'to shew not so much the increase in number, as the inward growth in knowledge and grace' of the Greenland congregation (Cranz, 1767 I, xi) and 'growth in depth' was a key strategy of the South African mission (Boon, 2015, 87)—and this suited several constituencies, including the expanding colonial state. Qualitative accounts of sweet, spontaneous or perfectly harmonious singing—contrasted with unflattering accounts of the indigenous music it was said to have replaced— were understood to indicate the fundamental moral and religious reform of the singers. Colonial governors heard this as a musical manifestation of the progress of the Christian 'civilising' mission. The missionary and colonial projects were in many ways intertwined, often acting in mutually beneficial ways. Most missionaries relied happily on the force and support of colonial officials, and 'God Save the King' and 'Rule Britannia' were sung as well as hymns. Missionaries often made their congregations express their gratitude to the colonial government, and they were highly effective advocates of loyalty to the British imperial centre, as Elizabeth Elbourne (2002) has pointed out. Missions were particularly important 'on the margins of empire' (Elbourne, 2002, 14): they often represented the first or primary contact with people at the colonial frontier, and they were crucially involved with 'the initial steps of imperial expansion' in the first half of the nineteenth century (Johnston, 2003, 13). Anna Johnston has emphasised that the missionary project pretended to represent 'a model of "civilised" expansionism and colonial community management' (ibid.). Missionaries seemed to offer a certain moral justification for imperialism, as they enabled colonial expansion to be framed as the noble progress of Christian civilisation, with what they saw as ignorant heathens remodelled into 'imperial archetypes of civility and modernity' (ibid.).

This view was especially prominent, around the turn of the nineteenth century, in abolitionist and antislavery discourse, which intersected strongly with evangelising and missionary ideas (see Vernal, 2012).

Latrobe himself was a strong opponent of slavery. He relied on rich and powerful abolitionist figures in his personal network—especially Beilby Porteous, Charles Middleton and Henry Thornton—for financial and political support for the Moravian mission, so he was often obliged to make this moral case quite strongly. He recounts in his diary several productive meetings with the leader of the abolitionist movement, the Member of Parliament William Wilberforce. On 7 January 1788 Wilberforce 'paid me an agreeable Visit, with a View to speak with me on the mode of converting the poor negroes on the [West] Coast of Africa to Christianity—hoping thereby to civilise them & make them useful to themselves' (Journal of Christian Ignatius Latrobe, 7 January 1788, f. 2). The two met again on 25 January 1788 and talked at length about them potential benefits of a mission in Guinea. According to Latrobe, Wilberforce stated his view that the Moravian missionaries 'would easily bring those of this poor nation, that would adopt the Christ[ian] Religion into a regular way of life, teaching them to till the ground, to plant Cotton & Indigo, articles much more valuable to this Country—than Slaves—to live in a regular Sociable manner … and thus, by introducing Civilisation & above all things true Christianity amongst them, make some amends to this nation for the Cruelties inflicted upon them' (ibid., 24 January 1788, ff. 4–5). Other diary entries show Wilberforce offering his support for Moravian missionary endeavours in St Kitts and at Botany Bay in Australia (ibid., 2 June and 16 July 1789, ff. 106–7). Wilberforce seems to have seen 'introducing Civilisation' and encouraging a 'regular way of life', according to the European model, as a means of making up for the injustices of the slave trade. Some abolitionists around the time of Latrobe's meetings with Wilberforce even invoked music in their attempts to garner support. William Dickson, for example, referred to 'The fondness of the negroes for music … [and] their taste for melody and harmony … as an argument in proving their humanity' (Dickson, 1789, 84). Latrobe knew that accounts of civilised and regular singing among African congregations and the (formerly) enslaved would strengthen the abolitionists' arguments and their crucial financial support for the Moravian mission.

This 'use of musicality to demonstrate humanity' (Ryan, 2021, 158) was an important part of the Moravian missionary project that Latrobe administered. Although it is true that Moravian missionaries contributed to the well-discussed ethnomusicological 'hunt for difference' in colonial contexts (see Agawu, 2003; Chikowero, 2015), they were also looking for examples of 'natural' or 'universal' musicality that could demonstrate the essential, shared humanity of their (future) congregations. Tsing (2005, 89) describes how the 'searcher for universal truths must establish an *axiom* of unity', emphasising 'Convergences [that] offer legitimacy and charisma to nascent categories'. In practice this was a highly partial 'hunt for sameness' in the colonial-missionary context, where evidence of shared humanity was found in examples of European-style musical performance among non-Europeans.

Latrobe inserted examples of shared musicality in the *Periodical Accounts*, such as this 'Extract of the Diary of the Mission of the United Brethren at Gnadenthal, near the Cape of Good Hope' for 11 July 1813:

> We have often had occasion to observe, that the Hottentots possess considerable talents for music. This is remarkably evident in the harmonious singing of the congregation, and especially when small companies get together to sing hymns. To-day Brother Schwinn reported another proof of it. Going to call at one of the houses, he overheard the Hottentot inhabitant performing on the violin, who not only played that difficult hymn tune *Come, Holy Ghost, Come, Lord, Our God*, (see Hymn-book, p. 65), without fault, but contrived, by double stops, to play a very good second to it. (PA VI 1814–17, 27–8)[2]

Here, 'proof' of Africans' natural musicality is an individual's ability to play a 'difficult' European hymn in a way that this missionary considered sophisticated or challenging. 'Double stops' refers here to a technique used on string instruments, such as the violin, where the player presses down two strings at the same time with the bow to produce two notes simultaneously. By doing so, violinists can play two parts of the music at the same time, essentially 'harmonising' with themselves. Latrobe scored the hymns in his hymn books with second and third parts printed in the treble staff, so this violinist may even have been performing Latrobe's arrangement, although the word 'contrived' here suggests that the violinist had to use some impressive ingenuity or creativity to make this work because the arrangement was not written with solo violin performance in

---

[2] In this period, white Europeans generally used the racial term 'Hottentot' to refer to the indigenous Khoekhoe, a nomadic pastoralist people in southwestern Africa. I have generally omitted this and other racist terms when quoting the nineteenth-century sources I use in this chapter. However, in some cases—as here—I quote such language directly as it indicates how these white writers used these terms to make general claims about an entire 'race' of people.

mind. Essentially, the ability to use harmony in this way was considered evidence of a natural musicality and even humanity.

On his own visit to the Gnadenthal mission in South Africa two years later, Latrobe himself made a similar observation and logical claim:

> To-day I heard with much pleasure a party of men and women, employed as day-labourers in the missionaries' garden, both before and after their meal, which they enjoyed in the shade of the grove, most melodiously singing a verse, by way of a grace. One of the women sung a correct second, and very sweetly performed that figure in music, called Retardation [here Latrobe includes a small sheet music image showing a feature often found in his own compositions and arrangements] from which I judge, that dissonants are not the invention of art, but the production of nature. Nothing would be more easy, than to form a chorus of the most delightful voices, in four parts, from among this smooth-throated nation. (Latrobe, 1818, 67)

Again, it is the ability to perform harmony with a second part that demonstrates this people's natural musicality, plus the skilful use of dissonant non-chord tones in a style that was common among European composers of the Classical era. Latrobe also extrapolates from this African musical performance that 'dissonants' are not a specific invention of European culture but are in fact a natural part of human musicality. Their possession of this skill means, for Latrobe, that it would be 'easy' to make further musical progress. Latrobe's son John Antes Latrobe made this argument—that 'harmonizing or performing in parts' was natural, God-given and deducible through experience and reason—more fully in his book on *The Music of the Church* (1831, 44–5). All this was part of the scaling up process and the production of scalability. The expansion of the colonial project and the expansion of the missionary project relied on each other, both practically and in terms of offering a kind of moral justification. The demonstration of success in reforming the heathen, and in establishing a shared humanity via shared musicality, was also important for the abolitionist movement, who provided moral, practical, financial and political support to the Moravians.

But for the Moravians to make their musical-culture project fully scalable, two problems remained: (1) the need for reliable and appropriate musical accompaniment (both instruments and musicians) to support the congregations' singing, and (2) the need to eradicate other, pre-existing or conflicting forms of music and musical culture. Solving both these problems would produce the scalability necessary for the musical methods that had proved successful to be applied more generally.

To take the second problem first: it is important to remember that, for Moravians, the use of music was not purely a practical means of building and extending the missions as institutions. For them, harmonious, European-style singing was evidence of the mission having produced truly reformed Christian believers who were closer to God and to a place in heaven. Latrobe and others thought that the universal, natural qualities of music were literally divine—a way of experiencing something of heaven on Earth. Latrobe (1790, ii) saw melodious, Christian singing as a 'gift of God bestowed upon us', and the missionaries presented it in this way to their congregations. Agawu (2016, 338) reflects critically on how colonisers' hymn-singing apparently 'promised access to some precious accoutrements of modernity and eventually a place in heaven'. Crucially, this emphasis on the heavenly nature of Moravian music came with strong denigration of other styles of music, both other secular European music and especially the musical cultures and rituals that the missionaries encountered and sought to stamp out. For Latrobe, the use of God-given music should be 'altogether confined to the service of religion' (PA IX 1823, 238), and it should not be 'abused' by being used for other purposes. Latrobe wrote that 'I have been taught most highly to value Music as a gift of God bestowed upon man for the noblest purposes, to regret its misapplication, and to abhor its abuse' (1828 I, iv). In a musical essay addressed to his daughter, Latrobe told her that her 'musical talent was given you, that you might in this state of trial and preparation have, for your encouragement, the means of enjoying a foretaste of that eternal bliss, wherein your occupation will be a perpetual expression of gratitude to Him … Under this impression, you will be tempted to use it for no other purpose than for the glory of our Savior' (quoted in *The Moravian Church Miscellany* IV 1853, 353). He seems to have taught his son the same thing, since a few years later John Antes Latrobe (1831, 151) criticised 'the mean and licentious ditties of the tavern, or the more refined but equally vain melodies of the opera—any thing, in short, that is inferior to the sublimest strains of our richest ecclesiastical harmonies'. John Antes Latrobe, as his father, considered it highly regrettable 'when the chief instrument of their elevation is accounted a mere tool of convenience, or amusement for the vulgar … By their own negligence, they incapacitate themselves from joining in the only mode of expressing the highest state of spiritual exultation' (ibid., 181).

Considering this attitude, widespread among Moravians, it is not surprising that missionary accounts used highly pejorative and critical language to describe the indigenous music they sought to replace. They denigrated dancing especially. Take, for example, this extract of a report on 'the beginning of the mission of the United Brethren, Among the Chippeway Indians, near Lake Erie, in Canada' that Latrobe published in the fourth volume of the *Periodical Accounts*:

> [T]he Indians held their autumnal dance [in late September 1802], a festivity observed with a view to a successful chase. Their drums resounded all night through. It cannot be described how these people are sunk in superstition, and how fast they are bound in the chains of satan. On these occasions, the sorcerers play the chief, and to themselves the most profitable, part. Oh, that the Lord would soon have mercy upon this nation! (PA IV 1806–10, 142)

A couple of months later, the missionary there was already making 'a trial to translate some hymns' (ibid., 145) as part of his first attempt to replace the 'superstitious' drum-based musical culture he found with melodious singing of European Christianity.

As non-Moravian music was outlawed at the mission stations, the missionaries reacted extremely severely when they discovered that the congregation had been dancing or musicking otherwise. The 10 June 1809 diary entry for the Gruenekloof mission in South Africa describes a particularly spectacular example of this. The missionaries had learnt that a member of the congregation named Klaas Trompeter had been inclined to

> entice women and children and others to come to his house and join in a dance, connected with the most superstitious and indecent practices. These abominations had existed for some time in darkness, till some of the school-children betrayed the party, by informing Sister Schmitt of it. On examination, we found that not only most of the scholars had joined in it, but even several women, and two of the candidates for baptism. We consulted together, how we might, with the help of God, at once put a stop to such dangerous and seductive practices, and prayed the Lord, in this distressing case, to give us grace, firmness, and success. On the following evening, Brother Kohrhammer ... declared their nocturnal dances, following immediately upon their assembling to hear the word of God, to be a work of the devil, by which the arch-enemy of souls seeks to destroy the good seed sown, that it may bring forth no fruit ... On the following day, the children came running to Brother and Sister Schmitt with tears and lamentations,

crying for forgiveness, promising never more to be guilty of such evil doings. The women came with the same professions of contrition to Brother and Sister Kohrhammer. This proved a seasonable opportunity of representing to them the abominably sinful and damnable nature of all their old heathen-ish superstitions and wanton practices, by which the devil leads them captive at his will, and to explain, how by these things the wrath of God comes upon all unbelievers. They were then permitted, by giving us their hands, sol-emnly to promise never to suffer themselves again to be seduced in these sinful ways. Klaas Trompeter, perceiving that his diabolical traffic was at an end, came at length himself, fell on his knees, and entreated us to forgive him. However, to him we could not speak as to those who had fallen into his snares, but as to an agent of the devil and wicked seducer. But he per-sisted to cry aloud for mercy, till we told him, that if he would bring his violin, with which he had set his wicked dance a-going, and deliver it up into custody, in token of his never encouraging these practices again, we should consider about it. He was overjoyed at this glimpse of hope of forgiveness, got up, ran home, took the old violin down, and exclaimed, 'Get out of the house, thou instrument of the devil!'—and brought it immediately to us, to keep for him as long as we pleased. Having once more represented to him the atrociousness of his former practices, we added, that though we forgave him, yet that this would not clear him of his guilt; for he must seek forgive-ness with God, who alone could save him from eternal punishment. Thus ended this distressing business; and we were glad to perceive, that a deep and salutary impression was made upon old and young. (PA V 1811–14, 62–4)

Although this was just one part of wider missionary efforts to reform African cultural rituals, gender roles, dress and so on (Tonono, 2019), it is hard to overstate the violence of this kind of spectacular episode in which music and dancing were represented as 'abominably sinful and damnable', with 'a deep and salutary impression' on the rest of the congregation. The *Periodical Accounts* report other, similar accounts in South Africa alone, such as when some prospective converts who had been 'very wild, and spent their time in fiddling and dancing' later 'broke their fiddles in pieces, and are now attentive hearers in all our meetings' (PA IX 1823, 38). Violent violin destruction happened in the nearby South African mission stations of the London Missionary Society too for similar reasons (see Elbourne, 2002, 187). This denigration of indigenous musicking was a key process of 'perceptual reform' (Robinson, 2020, 40) and the 'cultural disarmament' and 'alienation' (Chikowero, 2015) that musical colonisa-tion always entailed. Formally renouncing dancing and trivial music-making was, in missionaries' eyes, an important stage in the process of conversion from unworthy heathen to good Christian. According to the *Periodical Accounts*, members of the various Moravian mission congregations were often quick to renounce their old musical practices as sinful and shameful, and they were rewarded for doing so. This extinguishing of existing social 'entanglements' of various kinds in order to create pixel-like blocks devoid of transformative social relations is what Tsing (2012, 151) sees as a crucial stage in the production of scalability. The cultural landscape must be cleared, simplified and fundamentally remade, with the people alienated from their existing rituals, sounds and aesthetic preferences, for certain practices to become scalable.

The other obstacle to full scalability concerned the need for reliable and appropriate musical accompaniment (both instruments and musicians) to support the congregations' singing. It was common for missionaries to lament that their congregations apparently struggled to maintain the correct pitch. Cranz, for example, wrote of the Greenlanders: 'Their only fault is, that they are apt to let their voices sink, especially in a long metre, but this is remedied by the help of music' (Cranz, 1767 II, 423). Latrobe wrote in the introduction to his collection of *Hymn-Tunes* (1790, iii) that 'the natural imbecility of the human voice is such, that few can keep to the pitch in which a tune is begun, especially in long hymns, or a succession of many verses'. (Notice again that this flaw is apparently 'natural' and presumably shared by all.) For this reason, Latrobe dedicated a great deal of effort to finding the best musical instruments to export to the scattered mission stations, often stopping in at his favourite music shops in London to find a bargain for that purpose. He also addressed the voice-lowering issue, conducting experiments on his South African tour. He describes how he sat down to play piano one evening at a mission station, only to be joined by a few curious members of the congregation:

I told them, that I would play for *them*, but they should sing for *me*, as I wished to ascertain, whether, by the help of an instrument, they would keep true to the tune, without sinking their voices. They then gave out, and sung some verses, in different tunes; I always found them true to the pitch of the instrument, though every now and then I let them sing some lines by themselves, then falling in with the piano-forte, found they had not in the smallest degree lowered their voices. The number of singers gradually increased to thirty. I was pleased with this new proof of the naturally musical qualities of this nation, and was convinced, that the sinking of the voices at church, is only owing to bad precentors, but would be prevented by an organ. (Latrobe, 1818, 107; italics in original)

We see here, again, the search for 'natural' musicality, but in this case the realisation of natural talent relies on musical accompaniment, ideally from an organ.[3] Organs were 'undoubtedly of all other instruments best adapted' for this purpose (Latrobe, 1790, iii). Latrobe's strongly pro-organ position was partly a straightforward aesthetic preference, one that his son inherited. John Antes Latrobe (1831, 350) wrote: 'No instrument on earth can be compared to the organ for fulness [sic], majesty, richness, modulation, and condensation of sound; and no instrument seems therefore so suited to the exclusive adoration of Him ... Perhaps no work of man's device can claim equal power of exciting and arresting the feelings.' But there was also an issue of practicality and, indeed, scalability. Latrobe received several letters from the Labrador missionaries complaining that the various instruments he had sent previously, especially the wind instruments, would freeze and become unplayable in the colder months, so an organ, however small and cheap, would be gratefully received (see, e.g., PA VIII 1821–23, 96–7; 182–3). An organ was finally sent from Europe to Labrador in 1824. The congregation at New Fulnec in Jamaica gratefully received their organ in 1834, noting that 'it has a sweet tone, and we shall often thank you for it' (PA XIII 1834–36, 284). Elsewhere in the Moravian world, missionaries tried to construct their own organs. A small, home-made organ was debuted at the 1806 Christmas hymns at the Cherokee mission, for example, and it still 'accompanied the voices' in autumn 1808 (see PA IV 1806–10, 255; 379–80).[4]

Having a standard instrument that could be used in the vastly different contexts of the various Moravian missions was only a partial solution to the problem of accompaniment. There was also a need for trained

---

[3] It is notable that the later-nineteenth-century tonic sol-fa system that Olwage (2010) describes was designed to overcome this reliance on artificial accompaniment and instead find a way of restoring the naturally musical qualities of the human voice.

[4] The choice to export and/or construct a European instrument, rather than adapt the instruments already used by and widely available among the indigenous congregations, is another element of the pixel-like scalability that the Moravians aimed for. Many instruments in the African context, for example, reflected local metallurgical engineering skills and resource availability, but they had cosmological, spiritual or other cultural significance that meant the missionaries were inclined to suppress or replace them. On this, see Chikowero (2015, 3).

organists. Most Moravian missionaries had some musical training but few had the specific skills to take on what Latrobe saw as the vitally important role of the church organist. The organ, thought Latrobe, was commonly used in an 'improper' manner by the untrained musician who 'easily exposes his inattention and want of true devotion' (Latrobe, 1790, iii). John Antes Latrobe (1831, 366) emphasised 'the astonishing power reposed in the hands of the organist', the tenor of whose performance would ensure the religious enrichment or the regrettable dissipation of the congregation: 'He holds over them an enchanter's wand, powerful as the lightning, and almost equally destructive' (ibid., 366). The collection of hymn tunes that Latrobe sent around the missions contained important instructions for the (trainee) organist. Moravian organists should be extremely attentive to the singing of the congregation, taking care never to overpower but always playing with 'sufficient strength of sound to prevent their sinking' (Latrobe, 1790, vi). They should also be restrained and avoid the 'shakes, and other graces' that Latrobe so despised (ibid.). And, most importantly, whoever filled this important role should know all the hymns in the book by heart and 'should be able to play the hymn Tunes in most if not all the different keys extempore', following the rhythms and pauses of the singing, in order not to disrupt the sometimes spontaneous choices of the minister and congregation (ibid.). These instructions were distributed in successive editions of Latrobe's *Hymn-Tunes* throughout the nineteenth century, as a guide to how organists should be trained, both in Europe's seminaries and throughout the Moravian missionary world. By 1837, the Labrador congregation's singing was supported by 'an Eskimo brother, who is able to play most of the hymn tunes in use among us on the organ, and gladly assists in the services of the Church' (PA XIV 1836, 217). As early as 1835 the missionaries in South Africa were boasting that a young African man named Ezekiel Pfeiffer had 'begun to play the organ at the church, and is thus, in all probability, the first Hottentot organist in the world' (PA XIII 1834–6, 340). Here the racial term refers not specifically to a southern African group but rather reflects the fact that, by the eighteenth century, the word was a generic epithet for those considered barbarian or primitive, and as such the successful musical training of Pfeiffer represented the feasibility of employing indigenous musicians to accompany the singing at all the mission stations across the world. By 1838, Pfeiffer was 'our regular Organist' (PA XIV 1836, 325), accompanying the choir who had been trained to sing four-part harmonies. This achieved Latrobe's aim of forming a well-trained chorus from among the South African people (Latrobe, 1818, 67), with accompaniment on an instrument and in a style endorsed by him. Pfeiffer then helped train another African organist, Alexander Haas, who went as a 'native assistant' to another mission station in the colony in 1843. In this way, both the standardised musical instrument *and* the standardised skills and performance styles that Latrobe had instituted were scaled up across South Africa and beyond. At the different stations around the world, the policy increasingly became to train local members of the congregation according to Latrobe's advice, so that the instrument, the canon of tunes and the performance conventions were exported from Europe, embodied in the organ and the organist.

This was the musical production of scalability—a means of ensuring a favoured set of musical practices and materials did not need to be changed in order to be widely extended, expanded and reproduced. This entailed, on the one hand, standardising forms, instruments, tunes and performance styles. From producing and circulating books of translated hymns, to sending musical instruments that would work in any conditions, to selecting and training musicians according to a specific set of rules, the Moravian missionary project was based on a concerted effort to scale up a particular musical repertoire and a particular way of musicking. On the other hand, the Moravians' musical colonisation project also involved engineering the contexts of the circulation and performance of these musical forms, instruments, repertoires and styles by radically simplifying the cultural landscape in which they would be propagated. This large-scale standardisation relied on a concerted project of 'cultural alienation' and 'epistemicide' (Chikowero, 2015, 3–4)—outlawing and denigrating indigenous musicking, dancing, instruments and so on in order to produce the stable, standard, pixel-like units devoid of transformative social relations that were necessary for musical expansion. Latrobe and the other Moravian missionaries justified this by emphasising the elevated nature of their style of music, the divinity of which meant that any 'lower' use of music—for entertainment or socialisation, say—was to be severely regretted. Latrobe wrote that music should not be used in 'amusements for the vulgar', and in fact it should be heard 'for no other purpose' than for moving closer to heaven (Latrobe quoted in *The Moravian Church Miscellany* IV 1853, 353). His son similarly thought that 'every sound that is uttered should be a vehicle for divine communications' (John Antes Latrobe, 1831, 75). Replacing indigenous forms of musicking with what they saw as the only music worthy of human time and attention was an integral part of the Moravian project, and it was a way of scaling up the significance of music by placing it beyond 'this world' at the level of the heavenly or divine (Latrobe quoted in *The Moravian Church Miscellany* IV 1853, 349). But of course the supposedly divine features of music—those that apparently pointed to its large-scale spiritual significance—were in fact a quite particular set of features favoured by European evangelicals. It was these musical features that Latrobe and others looked for in the indigenous congregations they sought to convert, and it was these apparently 'natural' and even 'universal' musical features that they emphasised as evidence of the progress of European civilisation when they needed the support of colonial governors, and as evidence of a shared humanity when they sought support from abolitionists in Europe. Of course music was by no means the sole agent of colonisation in the places where the Moravians evangelised, but it worked in important relation with many of the practices of the colonial state, while functioning as a moral justification for imperial ideologies.

In 1831 John Antes Latrobe wrote that, with the great Classical European composers, music had 'reached its highest pitch of refinement' in a style that had been 'universally adopted among civilized nations' (John Antes Latrobe, 1831, 69). But as this chapter has shown, this universalisation of culture—in the Glissantian sense of *imposing or projecting one place into elsewhere*—required substantial scale-building effort.

References

Agawu, K. (2003). *Representing African music: Postcolonial notes, queries, positions.* Routledge.

Agawu, K. (2016). Tonality as a colonizing force in Africa. In R. Radano & T. Olaniyan (Eds.), *Audible empire: Music, global politics, critique* (pp. 334–355). Duke University Press.

Baker, G. (2008). *Imposing harmony: Music and society in colonial Cuzco.* Duke University Press.

Boon, P. G. (2015). *Hans Peter Hallbeck and the cradle of missions in South Africa: A theological-critical study.* PhD thesis, University of the Free State (Universiteit van die Vrystaat).

Chikowero, M. (2015). *African music, power, and being in colonial Zimbabwe.* Indiana University Press.

Cranz, D. (1767). *The history of Greenland: Containing a description of the country, and its inhabitants* (2 vols). Printed for the Brethren's Society for the Furtherance of the Gospel among the Heathen.

Dickson, W. (1789). *Letters on slavery*. J. Phillips.

Elbourne, E. (2002). *Blood ground: Colonialism, missions, and the contest for Christianity in the Cape Colony and Britain, 1799–1853*. McGill-Queen's University Press.

Eyerly, S. J. (2020). *Moravian soundscapes: A sonic history of the moravian missions in early Pennsylvania*. Indiana University Press.

Garofalo, R. (1993). Whose world, what beat: The transnational music industry, identity, and cultural imperialism. *The World of Music, 35*(2), 16–32.

Glissant, É. (2020). *Treatise on the whole-world* (C. Britton, Trans.). Liverpool University Press.

Goodman, G. (2012). 'But they differ from us in sound': Indian psalmody and the soundscape of colonialism, 1651–75. *The William and Mary Quarterly, 69*(4), 793–822.

Johnson-Williams, E. (2020). The examiner and the evangelist: Authorities of music and empire, c. 1894. *Journal of the Royal Musical Association, 145*(2), 317–350.

Johnston, A. (2003). *Missionary writing and empire, 1800–1860*. Cambridge University Press.

'Journal of Christian Ignatius Latrobe', January 1788–June 1789. Moravian Church Manuscripts, MS 1244. University of Manchester Library.

Latour, B. (1987). *Science in action: How to follow scientists and engineers through society*. Harvard University Press.

Latrobe, C. I. (1790). *Hymn-tunes, sung in the Church of the United Brethren*. Printed for the Author, by J. Bland.

Latrobe, C. I. (1818). *Journal of a visit to South Africa, in 1815, and 1816*. L.B. Seeley and R. Ackermann.

Latrobe, C. I. (1828). *Original anthems for one, two, or more voices adapted for private devotion or public worship, composed and the accompaniments arranged for the Piano Forte or Organ* (2 vols). Printed for the Author, No.19, Bartletts Buildings, Holborn.

Latrobe, J. A. (1831). *The music of the church considered in its various branches, congregational and choral: An historical and practical treatise for the general reader*. R.B. Seeley and W. Burnside.

Magubane, Z. (2004). *Bringing the empire home: Race, class, and gender in Britain and colonial South Africa*. University of Chicago Press.

Okigbo, A. C. (2010). Musical inculturation, theological transformation, and the construction of black nationalism in early South African choral music tradition. *Africa Today, 57*(2), 42–65.

Olwage, G. (2004). Discipline and choralism: The birth of musical colonialism. In A. J. Randall (Ed.), *Music, power, and politics* (pp. 33–54). Routledge.

Olwage, G. (2010). Singing in the Victorian world: Tonic sol-fa and discourses of religion, science and empire in the Cape Colony. *Muziki, 7*(2), 193–215.

Periodical Accounts Relating to the Missions of the Church of the United Brethren, Established Among the Heathen. Vols. 1–14. Printed for the Brethren's Society for the Furtherance of the Gospel. 1790–1836.

Robinson, D. (2020). *Hungry listening: Resonant theory for indigenous sound studies.* University of Minnesota Press.

Ryan, M. T. (2021). *Hearing power, sounding freedom: Black practices of listening, ear-training, and music-making in the British Colonial Caribbean.* PhD dissertation, University of Pennsylvania.

Schutt, A. C. (1999). Tribal identity in the Moravian missions on the Susquehanna. *Pennsylvania History: A Journal of Mid-Atlantic Studies, 66*(3), 378–398.

Stevens, C. E. (1971). *The musical works of Christian Ignatius Latrobe.* PhD dissertation, The University of North Carolina at Chapel Hill.

Straw, W. (1991). Systems of articulation, logics of change: Communities and scenes in popular music. *Cultural Studies, 5*(3), 368–388.

The Moravian Church Miscellany volume 4 (1853). Published for the Church of the United Brethren.

Tomlinson, J. (1991). *Cultural imperialism: A critical introduction.* Pinter Publishers.

Tonono, S. (2019). Uyajola 9/9 uTata'kho: Missionaries and black masculinities. *African Journal of Gender and Religion, 25*(2), 109–133.

Tsing, A. L. (2005). *Friction: An ethnography of global connection.* Princeton University Press.

Tsing, A. L. (2012). On nonscalability: The living world is not amenable to precision-nested scales. *Common Knowledge, 18*(3), 505–524.

Vernal, F. (2012). *The farmerfield mission: A Christian community in South Africa, 1838–2008.* Oxford University Press.

CHAPTER 6

From the Particulars to the General: A Small-Scale Conclusion

Abstract The main arguments and implications of the foregoing chapters are briefly summarised, emphasising how music has been involved in the normalisation or imposition of particular scalar relations, while also contesting dominant scalar systems and hierarchies.

Keywords Janelle Monáe • Wiley • Nadia Rose • Grime • Louis Armstrong • Climate protest • Édouard Glissant • Scalability • Universalism • Digital music

This book has analysed four examples that demonstrate the richness of music's engagement with scale. I have sought to show how diverse musical practices among diverse social groups can contribute to the cultural production of scale. The analysis of Janelle Monáe shows how pop musicians can be highly 'agile' in their use of scale, producing music that works at multiple scales while also subverting, splitting and reimagining the relationships between scales such as 'the body', 'the metropolitan' and 'the global'. In focusing on the work of Wiley and Nadia Rose, I have indicated how the intensely local or postcode-scale aesthetics of grime music are part of a socio-political strategy that draws attention to mechanisms of inclusion and exclusion, potentially remaking the borders of 'the local' when the genre's political potential is heard by particular listeners. The use of a Louis Armstrong classic as a climate protest song shows the potential of musical 'scale jumping', reorienting audiences to new scales of political contest and musically fusing relations between the experiential and the general, or between particular places and what Glissant calls the 'Whole-World'. Finally, missionaries' processes of musical colonialism can be better understood when framed in terms of the cultural production of scalability, with historical attention to the efforts involved in musical scale-building projects that make claims about music's universal qualities.

Through these varied analyses, I have sought to show how music has been involved in the normalisation or imposition of particular scalar relations, while also contesting dominant scalar systems and hierarchies. In theorising and critically reflecting on ideas of scale in relation to music, the book has drawn attention to something that many music scholars use commonly but generally uncritically. I hope I have demonstrated the value of addressing the role of music in the production of scale, although much more remains to be done: from understanding the role of digitally produced music in the scaling of the digital world, to tracing longer histories and remnants of musical scalability projects. Crucially, I have argued that researchers of music should not just adopt in advance the scalar frames with which music is analysed, nor apply musical scales as metaphors for geographical ones. Instead, the task for music researchers is to explore scale *through* music, and to appreciate the sophistication of music's own scale-making practices. After all, we already live in a world whose scales are made by music, but music also has the potential to produce a world scaled otherwise.

Index[1]

[1] Note: Page numbers followed by 'n' refer to notes.

© The Author(s) 2023   105

P. Dodds, *Music and the Cultural Production of Scale*,

https://doi.org/10.1007/978-3-031-36283-5

The manufacturer's authorised representative in the EU is Springer
Nature Customer Service Centre GmbH, Europaplatz 3, 69115 Heidelberg,
Germany. If you have any concerns regarding our products, please
contact ProductSafety@springernature.com

Printed and bound by CPI Group (UK) Ltd, Croydon, CR0 4YY

29/04/2026

02099525-0004